PRAISE FOR
THE SEVEN DECISIONS

"Andy Andrews' words—both written and spoken—are a significant and enduring presence in the lives of our Squadron Commanders around the world."

—LT. GEN. MICHAEL W. WOOLEY
USAF COMMANDER, AIR FORCE SPECIAL OPERATIONS COMMAND

"Andy teaches with humor and stories . . . the best way for most to learn the lessons that can change your business . . . and your life."

—RHONDA FERGUSON
PRESIDENT, FINANCIAL CONCEPTS

"My friend Andy Andrews is an inspiration! Read this book and find out for yourself."

—REBECCA LUKER
BROADWAY STAR

"If you are struggling with a troubled past or an uncertain future, this book can lead you to triumph."

—JOHN STARR
CEO, KOCH EQUIPMENT, LLC, MEMBER OF YPO

"*The Seven Decisions* manages to practically address life's challenging balance between taking action and simply trusting God."

—JOSH JENKINS
PRESIDENT & CEO, TREEHOUSESEM.COM AND ENSURE CHARITY

"*The Seven Decisions* seamlessly unites life elements that are difficult to pull off on their own, much less together."

—ZACH SMITH
PRESIDENT, MERCHANTPLUS

THE SEVEN DECISIONS

UNDERSTANDING THE KEYS TO PERSONAL SUCCESS

ANDY ANDREWS

W PUBLISHING GROUP

AN IMPRINT OF THOMAS NELSON

Published in Nashville, Tennessee, by W Publishing Group, an imprint of Thomas Nelson.

Thomas Nelson titles may be purchased in bulk for educational, business, fund-raising, or sales promotional use. For information, please e-mail SpecialMarkets@ThomasNelson.com.

Scripture quotations marked KJV are from the King James Version of the Bible.

Scripture quotations marked NIV are from the Holy Bible, New International Version®, NIV®. © 1973, 1978, 1984 by Biblica, Inc.™ Used by permission of Zondervan. All rights reserved worldwide.

ISBN 978-0-529-10435-9 (repack)

Library of Congress Cataloging-in-Publication Data

Andrews, Andy, 1959–
   The seven decisions: understanding the keys to personal success / Andy Andrews.
   pages cm.
   Includes bibliographical references.
      ISBN 978-0-7852-6141-4
   1. Conduct of life. 2. Success. 3. Andrews, Andy, 1959– Traveler's gift. I. Title.
BJ1581.2.A535 2008
158.1—dc22   2007039924

Printed in the United States of America

14 15 16 17 18 RRD 5 4 3 2 1

To Maryann and Jerry Tyler of Roswell, Georgia

*I am so grateful for the love, wisdom, belief, patience, and example
you have shown me throughout the years.*

Contents

CONTENTS

CONTENTS

PREFACE

When my book *The Traveler's Gift* was released in 2002, no one knew what to expect. After all, even the bookstores could not decide upon the section in which the book would be displayed. Neither, evidently, could the media.

As ABC's *Good Morning America* promoted the book, it began to appear on every bestseller list in the country. *The Traveler's Gift* was on the *New York Times* list in the Fiction category. At the same time the *Wall Street Journal* listed it as *Non*fiction. It was Self-Improvement at Barnes & Noble, Literature on Amazon.com, Religion in *Publisher's Weekly*, and General Content in *USA Today*. Finally the *New York Times* changed *The Traveler's Gift* to its Advice list, back to Fiction, and lastly to the Business list, where it stayed for seventeen weeks.

I was not really surprised by the confusion. Twenty-five years of researching these Seven Decisions have not made them easier for me to label. They do, however, prove their value every time I personally put one to work or observe them in the lives of others.

Can you imagine? Every single time I have harnessed or watched someone harness these decisions, they work! Why? Because they're principles . . . and principles always work.

What you are about to read is not a work based on seven ideas or seven theories. These are not seven habits. They aren't even mine! I didn't invent or discover them. I merely identified them and have spent more than twenty-five years of personal research proving their value. So as you read, be aware that principles work every time—and they work whether you know them or not.

I have come to the conclusion that the principles of personal success—parenting, relationships, financial achievement—are floating around just like the principle of gravity. Therefore, why shouldn't we learn them and harness them to create the future of our choosing?

Get ready to have fun . . . and let's get started!

Andy Andrews

Orange Beach, Alabama

CREATING THE LIFE YOU CHOOSE

DISCOVERING THE SEVEN DECISIONS

In *The Traveler's Gift*, the main protagonist, David Ponder, finds himself in a difficult predicament: he's lost his job, his twelve-year-old daughter is sick, and he can't afford to pay for treatment. After a devastating car crash, Ponder is teleported to an adventure of discovery where he meets seven prominent historical figures, each of whom gives Ponder a separate decision he can make that will change his life.

We're not all so fortunate to be offered an escape from the pain and drama of life. I know I wasn't. I grew up in a typical middle-class family—my parents loved me, I loved them, and life was great . . . until I turned nineteen. Then, in a one-two punch that sent me reeling, my mom died of cancer and my dad was killed in a car accident.

Obviously, I was devastated. My confusion and grief quickly

turned into anger. I didn't have a lot of extended family or friends to lean on for support; therefore I managed to take a terrible situation and make it infinitely worse. Because I was filled with bitterness and unanswerable questions, a series of bad choices led me to a life of homelessness (at least a decade before "homeless" was even a word). No one from whom to borrow fifty dollars, no house, no car, no job, and, seemingly, no future. You can read much more about this journey in my book *The Noticer.*

Often spending nights under the state pier in my newly adopted hometown of Gulf Shores, Alabama, and in and out of the garages of unknowing homeowners, I bitterly remembered an old adage from childhood: "God will put a man after His own heart where He wants him to be." I remember thinking, *Thanks. You put me under a pier.*

Feeling desperate and helpless, I couldn't shake this one question, and it relentlessly plagued my mind: *Is life just a lottery ticket?*

How does person A end up with a healthy family and a job he loves, while person B ends up living under a pier? Does life come down to the luck of the draw? *If life is indeed a lottery ticket,* I thought, *and this is my ticket, perhaps I might just quit.* These were my first thoughts of suicide.

Man, I would have felt lucky to be teleported somewhere . . . anywhere! Instead, I was doing odd jobs, like cleaning fish and washing boats, and I had a lot of time on my hands that I often passed at the library. My free library card was my ticket to a new dimension—a world of endless possibilities, filled with extraordinary heroes from all walks of life.

At the suggestion of an old man who appeared out of nowhere one day, over the next couple of years, I read between two and three hundred biographies of happy, successful, influential people who, in their unique ways, changed the world. Some of these individuals amassed fortunes, but money wasn't what inspired me about them.

I wanted to find people who enjoyed contentment, happiness, and success in life as parents, friends, business owners, or leaders.

Somewhere in that library, my self-pity turned to passion. I was on a mission to find out how they did it. What was special about *them*? How did they end up so lucky? Did they do something specific? Follow a formula? Was it their religion or social standing? I wanted to believe that life wasn't just a lottery ticket, influenced by a roll of the dice. I read that Albert Einstein didn't like the idea of random chance—the notion that God played dice—so who was I to disagree with Einstein?

SEEK, AND YE SHALL FIND

Ask, and it shall be given you; seek, and ye shall find; knock, and it shall be opened unto you.

—MATTHEW 7:7 KJV

The first fifty biographies I read included Winston Churchill, George Washington Carver, Joshua Chamberlain, Will Rogers, Joan of Arc, Abraham Lincoln, and Viktor Frankl. I began to notice patterns—common threads that appeared to be woven through each historical account. These great men and women perceived the world in a similar way and were driven by similar belief systems with similar principles that guided their actions and interactions with the world.

I hunted intensely for clues, curiously discovering seven factors—seven clearly identifiable principles—that were embodied by each person, revealed in a diverse range of biographical accounts.

In some cases, these seven principles were inspired by arduous circumstances; in others, the individual seemed to learn the principles as children.

I wondered if I would be able to live these principles daily, even though I hadn't learned of them early in life. What if *I* mastered them? Would *my life* be worth writing about one day?

That day I became a lab rat in my own experiment that continues to this very moment. Over the next twenty years, I spent every day integrating the Seven Decisions into my life, and talking about them with others. I've had friends say, "Well, you have certainly been successful because of these Seven Decisions." I suppose one's perception of my success depends upon one's definition, but I can tell you this: *for some reason, I have become one of the greatest audiences to success the world has ever seen.*

For various reasons, I've had the opportunity to spend time with four different U.S. presidents. I've talked quietly with Bob Hope by his backyard swimming pool. I've walked through the woods with General Norman Schwarzkopf. I've hung out on buses with Garth Brooks, Kenny Rogers, and Randy Travis, and spent time backstage with Cher and Joan Rivers in Las Vegas. I've eaten lunches with Bart Starr, walked golf courses with Nancy Lopez, and eaten breakfast privately in Dublin with the director of the FBI while Gerry Adams, leader of the Irish Republican Army, waited for us in the next room.

Being a firm believer that the quality of our answers is determined by the quality of our questions, I have used these opportunities to ask what I believe are some great ones. I wanted to ask questions that would either confirm what I already knew or lead me to a broader definition of the truth. I asked questions like these:

- What's the first thing you do when you're depressed?
- What's the most important decision you've ever made in your life?
- What's the worst decision you've ever made in your life?

- If you were to give an eighteen-year-old one specific piece of wisdom, what would it be?
- What's the smartest thing your parents ever did?
- What's the last thing you do before you go to bed?
- What difference did someone make in your life as a child?

Over and over again I have confirmed that the Seven Decisions weave their way through the lives of successful people.

When *The Traveler's Gift* was published in November 2002, these Seven Decisions gained a very large audience. My experiment with these Decisions has expanded to include well over a million individual experiments by men and women worldwide who are integrating the Seven Decisions into their lives. Each week I am blessed with stories from all kinds of people who related to David Ponder's plight and experienced a turnaround in their lives as a consequence of living the Seven Decisions.

SEVEN PRINCIPLES, SEVEN DECISIONS

Remember, these Seven Decisions work *every time*. In fact, they are affecting your life right now whether you are aware of them or not. As we'll discuss, our thoughts carve a pathway to our success or failure. Our thoughts are determined by how well we understand these principles, so we'll go into some depth to explain and demonstrate these Seven Decisions in order to help you find distinctions that will enable you to create the you that you've always wanted to be!

You've heard "ignorance of the law is no excuse"? Well, ignorance of principle is no protection from that principle. Just because a person is unaware of a particular principle doesn't mean that principle is not affecting his life. After all, the principle of gravity worked long before the apple fell on Sir Isaac Newton's head. But once Newton understood the principle, mankind was able to harness the power of that principle to create airline flight, suspension bridges, and space travel.

Similarly, the principles of successful parenting, relationships, and financial achievement also work every time. And they can be harnessed by us all. By learning and applying them, obviously, we can create the future of our choosing!

Consider the effect of one principle, such as consistently taking responsibility for our own lives. How would one's life experience improve? Now, as powerful as one principle might be, imagine the power of seven principles stacked together! The result of grouping these seven life-changing principles into a common force bypasses minor, incremental changes to create an exponential explosion. Your life and the lives of those around you will be transformed as a consequence of mastering the Seven Decisions.

Before we begin in depth, here are the Seven Decisions that determine personal success:

One: The Responsible Decision

The buck stops here. I accept responsibility for my past. I am responsible for my success. I will not let my history control my destiny.

The Responsible Decision shows us how to stop blaming other people and outside circumstances for where we are in life. Instead, we can chart our life's course, allowing our lives to become testaments to the true power of choice.

Two: The Guided Decision

I will seek wisdom. God moves mountains to create the opportunity of His choosing. It is up to me to be ready to move myself.

The Guided Decision helps us discover invaluable counsel through books, people, and service. We learn to evaluate the network of influential people in our lives, to seek wisdom from the knowledge of others, and, perhaps most important, to commit to a life of service.

Three: The Active Decision

I am a person of action. Many people move out of the way for a person on the run; others are caught up in his wake. I will be that person on the run!

The Active Decision is a wake-up call. Taking consistent action is crucial to the realization of a successful life. We are often amazed, even baffled, by the accomplishments of highly successful people, yet many of their accomplishments occur because of relentless action.

Four: The Certain Decision

I have a decided heart. Criticism, condemnation, and complaint are creatures of the wind. They come and go on the wasted breath of lesser beings and have no power over me.

With the Certain Decision, we learn to break through fear and judgment to pursue our dreams with determination and focus. With a decided heart, we set our course and assure our destiny.

Five: The Joyful Decision

Today I will choose to be happy. My very life is fashioned by choice. First I make choices. Then my choices make me.

The Joyful Decision is perhaps the most misunderstood of all the Decisions. The Joyful Decision demonstrates that happiness is a choice, and if you are not happy right now, it is a consequence of your own choosing, not the circumstances of life.

Six: The Compassionate Decision

I will greet this day with a forgiving spirit. I know that God rarely uses a person whose main concern is what others are thinking.

The Compassionate Decision can heal your heart, mind, and

soul. Harboring anger and resentment poisons our minds and hinders our ability to live the other six Decisions with any measure of effectiveness. Forgiveness frees our spirits.

Seven: The Persistent Decision

I will persist without exception. Reason can only be stretched so far, but faith has no limits. The only limit to my realization of tomorrow is the doubt to which I hold fast today.

The Persistent Decision reveals a critical twist to the notion of persistence: persisting "without exception" is key to achieving extraordinary levels of success in any area of life. When we consistently make the Persistent Decision, our success is boundless.

REAL-LIFE TRAVELERS

To this day, I love reading biographies.

In the late 1980s, I took a more active approach to my Success Study. In addition to reading biographies and interviewing some extraordinary souls, I asked myself, *What if I could contact successful people—even those I don't know—and ask them to share with me their secrets to success and their strategies for overcoming rejection and failure?*

I began to compile a collection of what has become hundreds of personal letters from successful people in media, sports, business, art, and politics. Modern-day icons like General Chuck Yeager, Norman Vincent Peale, Dale Earnhardt, Sugar Ray Leonard, Bobby Bowden, Elizabeth Taylor, Mike Eruzione, and Orville Redenbacher all shared a few of their victories and many of their greatest defeats with me.

Not surprisingly, the principles from the Seven Decisions echoed throughout the letters, further confirming the study. To deepen your understanding of each Decision, I've combed through hundreds of these letters and provided edited versions of seven letters that I feel best personify each Decision to share with you.

THE QUALITIES OF LEADERSHIP

General George S. Patton, who served in both world wars, said, "Be willing to make decisions. That's the most important quality in a good leader."

As you read about the Seven Decisions, you will find that I did not use the word *leadership* very often, but everything discussed in this book reinforces the principles of leadership. The Seven Decisions will help you become the leader you were meant to be.

Leadership, or your ability to lead, is absolutely crucial to having the life you want. However, in my opinion, leadership as a course or study is overblown, overcomplicated, and a stumbling block to a lot of people. You do not have to read a thousand books on leadership to become a competent leader.

The secret to leadership is simple. You have within you the qualities you need to lead people—you only need to recognize them and begin using them. Our beliefs create our success or failure. Begin thinking differently about the leader you already are, and you alter your destiny.

It's amazing to me how many people come up to me after I have talked on the Seven Decisions and lament, "I'm really not a natural leader."

LEADERSHIP, OR YOUR ABILITY TO LEAD, IS ABSOLUTELY CRUCIAL TO HAVING THE LIFE YOU WANT. . . . THE SECRET TO LEADERSHIP IS SIMPLE. YOU HAVE WITHIN YOU THE QUALITIES YOU NEED TO LEAD PEOPLE—YOU ONLY NEED TO RECOGNIZE THEM AND BEGIN USING THEM.

I say, "Oh yes, you are! You are absolutely a natural leader."

Most people think, *Well, I don't have leadership qualities.*

Yes. Yes, you do!

It is important you understand this before we move into the Seven Decisions.

Leadership essentially boils down to two things: your perspective or beliefs about yourself, and a quality we can call "like-ability." Like-ability can be defined as the ability to build rapport so that others listen to you. We listen to the people we like.

You are already a natural leader. Everyone has led someone, even if that someone is a child. Leadership, to a great degree, is simply relating your beliefs or opinions to others with conviction and then sticking to that conviction, even in the face of criticism or dissent.

How many times have you been hanging with friends and somebody says, "Where do you want to eat?"

"I don't know. Where do *you* want to eat?"

All it takes is for one person to say, "McDonald's. Let's go to McDonald's."

The group likely responds, "Okay."

Have you ever noticed that there is one person in your group who inevitably decides what movie the group will see? Or at what restaurant the group will eat?

There are basically two reasons for this: first, everybody likes this person, and second, this person says something! He expresses his opinion. Everyone usually acquiesces. You may not consider that leadership, but that's exactly what leadership is!

These Seven Decisions are a basic course in becoming a person others want to be around and then increasing your influence. They will make you a more influential leader than any book on leadership skills, persuasion, closing techniques, or sales scripts, and they will help you find a platform for applying all you have learned.

Books and seminars on sales, leadership skills, and closing techniques are important, but without the implementation of these Seven Decisions, they honestly do not matter. You can know the "right" answer, have every word memorized, and know every statistic by heart, but if other people don't want to be around you or don't respect you, all the right answers in the world really don't matter. The Seven Decisions are the foundation for any other business improvement education. Although you will rarely find the word *leadership* as you move through these Seven Decisions, keep in mind that these principles will help you become the leader your children, spouse, coworkers, and friends deserve.

How to Read This Book

I have written this book for one purpose: to help you master the Seven Decisions that determine personal success. Most of us don't have the time to read several hundred biographies in order to clearly understand how successful people from all walks of life have lived these seven principles. *The Seven Decisions* is your personal owner's manual for crafting the life you want with a greater level of fulfillment.

And since I have mentioned it a couple of times already, let me say that reading *The Traveler's Gift* is not a prerequisite for benefiting from this book (though I do believe the story will create greater excitement for the journey you are about to take). For your convenience, the actual Seven Decisions David Ponder received from the seven historical figures are included. For each Decision, you will be presented with a series of exercises I often use in "The Seven Decisions Seminar." These exercises will help you further integrate the Decisions into your daily life.

A word of caution: Most of us tend to read passively. We sit back or lie down and scan the pages in a trancelike fashion. Although this style may be appropriate for pleasure reading, it is not the optimal style for processing this information. (Wouldn't it be nice if this information could be absorbed through osmosis by placing the book on our heads while we sleep at night?)

To support your comprehension of this information, a more active reading style would serve you better. What does this mean?

- rereading certain sections that resonate with you
- highlighting, underlining, and marking up the pages as you read
- completing the exercises in a pad or a journal (possibly more than once)
- consistently practicing the multiple-day exercises

Consider that these Seven Decisions aren't difficult to comprehend. In fact, one of the reasons many people do not consciously live the Decisions is because they appear too simple. *Surely the answers to life must be more complex than this!* This sentiment leads us to discount simple truths.

You may decide to read this book straight through before doing the exercises, or you may go "deep" with each Decision, completing each exercise before moving on to the next section. Whatever your preference, please make sure you do the exercises. Reading the text is simply not enough. Completing the exercises, even repeating them, will help you master all Seven Decisions. *The Seven Decisions* is an experiential learning course, reference manual, and companion for your journey toward the life you want.

I also recommend completing the exercises in a bound notebook or journal, rather than on scraps of paper, in order to have an ideal companion for future reference. I suggest investing in a leather-bound journal—something in which you will enjoy capturing your lifelong dreams, goals, creative ideas, memories, and life lessons. Yes, you could also do this on a computer or tablet, but there is something intrinsically powerful about a nice personal journal. That said, whatever works best for you, do that!

THE POWER OF CONSISTENCY

Lasting success is attainable by all of us. It's likely you've made each of the Seven Decisions at least once in your life. Although simple to understand, the Decisions aren't necessarily easy to carry out; however, the secret to lifelong success is in the *consistent* application of the Seven Decisions.

Our tendency is to try something a few times, and if it works, it gets reinforced, and we continue to do it; if it doesn't work, we abandon it. In psychology this is called the law of effects—we tend to keep doing things we are rewarded for doing. The opposite, however, is also true: we tend to avoid what punishes us or gives us pain.

Consciously applying the Seven Decisions consistently can be challenging at first. After all, although we may not love our life, it is at least familiar—and familiarity tends to breed comfort (even if that means being comfortable with massive debt, an unfulfilling job, or a contentious relationship).

It is helpful to view "decision making" not as a skill but as a muscle. Consider weight training: When you first try lifting a weight you are not accustomed to lifting—say, fifty pounds—it's difficult. Even if you complete a few reps, it's likely your body will later feel sore from stretching the muscle. For many of us, the challenge of lifting that fifty pounds and the soreness that follows is enough to keep us out of the gym. If, however, your commitment transcends your temporary discomfort, you will repeatedly lift the fifty pounds until it is easier, causing the pain and soreness to disappear as your body adapts. In time, through consistent effort, mastery is achieved: lifting fifty pounds is a breeze because it is within your domain of competence.

The consistent application of the Seven Decisions brings about what can be likened only to miracles: What was once labeled "impossible" becomes reality. Opportunities that once eluded you are now attracted to you. Dysfunctional relationships transform into harmonious ones. Life, which was once a struggle, now becomes an exciting adventure. Where you once perceived limitations, you now see possibilities. You go from "pushing" your way through life to "allowing" life's gifts to present themselves. You become a person others want to be around—a mentor, guide, and leader. The changes that arise have an infectious effect on those close to you: your spouse, family, friends, and coworkers; even people you meet in the elevator or supermarket are all uplifted by the person you have become by living the Seven Decisions.

The rewards of embracing the Seven Decisions are beyond measure—it is important to keep this in mind during the initial, arduous stages of the journey. This is, after all, where difficulties are likely to arise. Trust that the Decisions will not fail you. Through the consistent application and diligent effort of these Seven Decisions, you will discover abundant success!

ONE

THE RESPONSIBLE DECISION

THE BUCK STOPS HERE.

*If decisions are choices . . . and our thinking dictates our
decisions—then we are where we are because of our thinking.*

*The Responsible Decision for Personal Success is a key—it
represents the beginning. Taking responsibility for your past
will segue you into an extraordinary future of your choosing.*

THE BUCK STOPS HERE.

From this moment forward, I will accept responsibility for my past. I understand that the beginning of wisdom is to accept the responsibility for my own problems and that by accepting responsibility for my past, I free myself to move into a bigger, brighter future of my own choosing.

Never again will I blame my parents, spouse, boss, or employees for my present situation. Neither my education nor lack of one, my genetics, or the circumstantial ebb and flow of everyday life will affect my future in a negative way. If I allow myself to blame these uncontrollable forces for my lack of success, I will be forever caught in a web of the past. I will look forward. I will not let my history control my destiny.

The buck stops here. I accept responsibility for my past. I am responsible for my success.

I am where I am today—mentally, physically, spiritually, emotionally, and financially—because of decisions I have made. My decisions have always been governed by my thinking. Therefore, I am where I am today—mentally, physically, spiritually, emotionally, and financially—because of how I think. Today I will begin the process of changing where I am—mentally, physically, spiritually, emotionally, and financially—by changing the way I think.

My thoughts will be constructive, never destructive. My mind will live in the solutions of the future. It will not dwell in the problems of the past. I will seek the association of those who are working and striving to bring about positive changes in the world. I will never seek comfort by associating with those who have decided to be comfortable.

When faced with the opportunity to make a decision, I will make one. I understand that God did not put in me the ability to always make right decisions. He did, however, put in me the ability to *make* a decision and then make it right. The rise and fall of my emotional tide will not deter me from my course. When I make a decision, I will stand behind it. My energy will go into making the decision. I will waste none on second thoughts. My life will not be an apology. It will be a statement.

The buck stops here. I control my thoughts. I control my emotions.

In the future, when I am tempted to ask the question "Why me?" I will immediately counter with the answer, "Why *not* me?" Challenges are a gift, an opportunity to learn. Problems are the common thread running through the lives of great men and women. In times of adversity, I will not have a problem to deal with; I will have a choice to make. My thoughts will be clear. I will make the right choice. Adversity is preparation for greatness. I will accept the preparation. Why me? Why *not* me? I will be prepared for something great!

I accept responsibility for my past. I control my thoughts. I control my emotions. I am responsible for my success.

The buck stops here.

PLAYING THE BLAME GAME

If you want to hear a great fight, just turn on talk radio. They're relentless, those show hosts.

One side says, "These people need to accept responsibility, and until these people accept responsibility . . ."

The other side replies, "But it's not their fault. They're not to blame. Don't you understand . . . ?"

Both sides present a persuasive argument, but both sides are wrong.

Who or what do we blame? We blame our parents. We blame the weather. We blame the economy. We blame the president. We blame our spouses. It's amazing who we think of to blame.

Where I am today, we tell ourselves, *is a consequence of what other people* [our parents, for example] *and circumstances have done to me*. In blaming other people and events, we weaken our power. We argue, "It's not my fault . . ." As soon as we subscribe to this line of thinking, our chances for any kind of success dramatically decline.

When I was at my all-time low—homeless, living under a pier—I remember somebody telling me, "Well, you chose this." At first, that infuriated me. I remember thinking, *I didn't choose this. If my parents hadn't died, if there had been more insurance, if someone had helped me, if only . . .*

The problem with this line of thinking is that if you don't accept responsibility for where you are right now, you have no hope of changing your future. I promise you: if it is the president's fault, if it is your neighbor's fault, if it is your spouse's fault, if it is the government's fault, if it is the weather's fault, then you are truly stuck! What are you going to do about the president? What are you going to do about the weather? What can you do about your neighbor? I'll tell you: *nothing*! But if you can find the answer to your problems in the mirror—if the solution lies within you—well, there is boundless hope because you can start working on yourself today!

What most of the people on talk radio don't seem to understand is that responsibility is not about blame or making you feel bad about your situation. Responsibility is about hope and control. You feel more hopeful when you spread this vastly different perspective about responsibility—you can control your future! Who among us doesn't want a better future? These Seven Decisions can give you a better tomorrow by affecting the choices you make today.

Your day of reckoning is important. You must come to the self-realization that even though you couldn't control any of the crazy things that have happened in your life, your choices in response to those things are what have led you down this path you don't like.

We have the power to make choices that lead us to places we do not like. And that's great news! If we can make choices that lead us to places we don't like, then doesn't it stand to reason that we can also make choices that will lead us to a place we *do* like? If where we are today is not in our control, then how can tomorrow's fate be better? The game, then, becomes simple: *make better choices.*

We make our own way. Now that you are completely aware of this, you can claim it, make the decision to take responsibility, and begin living the Responsible Decision: *I am responsible for my past and my future.*

Why is that important? Until we accept responsibility for where we are, we have no basis for moving forward in our lives.

THE POWER OF THOUGHT

The Responsible Decision is all about owning our power. In a way, our choices have made us what we are today. And fundamentally, our *thinking*—the internal lens through which we see the world—creates a pathway to success or failure. To accept responsibility for our choices includes becoming aware of and accepting responsibility for our thinking. This clarification gives us the basis for moving on.

People sometimes question this idea. "Now, how does my thinking create a pathway for success or failure?" Despite what you may believe, outside influences are not responsible for where you are in life mentally, physically, spiritually, emotionally, or financially. You alone have chosen the path to your present destination.

TO ACCEPT RESPONSIBILITY FOR OUR CHOICES
INCLUDES BECOMING AWARE OF AND ACCEPTING
RESPONSIBILITY FOR OUR THINKING.

Decisions are an outward expression of our thinking. Most people agree that their decisions have guided them to where they are. If you want to create a pathway to the success you have dreamed of, rather than the reality you are currently experiencing, change your thinking.

You are where you are because of how you think. If you are in a bad place financially, physically, emotionally, socially, or spiritually, what does that tell you? Think about it: Nobody sets out to fail. Nobody says, "I'm going to make every bad decision I can possibly make."

Instead we say, "I'm going to figure this out. I'm going to do the right thing."

And yet we often end up in a horrible place in spite of ourselves! How does this happen? In many cases, our thinking got us here.

The primary way our thinking must change is to realize *we are responsible for where we are*. If we are responsible for where we are, we have hope! If we are responsible for where we are, then we can be responsible for where we're going. By disowning responsibility for our present, we give our power away and deny ourselves an incredible future.

We are often tempted to think, *Well, this is not my fault.* The words *It's not my fault* should never again come from your mouth! They have been symbolically written on the gravestones of unsuccessful people ever since Adam and Eve took the first bite of that apple.

Until we take responsibility for where we are, there is no basis for moving on. By taking responsibility, we have hope.

RESPONSIBLE THINKING

What thoughts do you have on a regular basis that may be leading you to an unhappy state of mind? Very often these thoughts take the form of defeated questions. For example: "Why am I so fat?" is not a question that will help you understand what steps to take to change your situation. However, "How can I enjoy sculpting my ideal body and reclaiming my energy?" will move you in the direction you want to go.

What questions do you habitually ask that are hindering your growth?

In a notebook or journal, list the unsupportive thoughts you often think. Then cross out each thought and restate it in a way that empowers you to obtain what you actually want.

CATCHING THE PRIZE

In the 1920s, a well-known, wealthy industrialist controlled a vast portion of our country's prosperity, and with his wealth he purchased a zoo. It wasn't a public zoo or even a private zoo; it was his personal zoo, located on his estate, for the pleasure of this one man and his family. National dignitaries were occasionally allowed to view the animals. In the days before zoo-breeding programs traded animals, his zoo was one of the most complete collections the zoological world had ever known. (During this time, zookeepers traveled to various countries, mounted safaris, and captured the animals to bring them back.)

One day he heard about a rare and beautiful type of gazelle from Africa that wasn't showcased in any zoo in the world. He became obsessed with the idea of becoming the first to have one of these animals in his collection.

WHEN FACED WITH THE OPPORTUNITY TO MAKE
A DECISION, I WILL MAKE ONE. I UNDERSTAND
THAT GOD DID NOT PUT IN ME THE ABILITY
TO ALWAYS MAKE RIGHT DECISIONS. HE DID,
HOWEVER, PUT IN ME THE ABILITY TO *MAKE*
A DECISION AND THEN MAKE IT RIGHT.

He mounted an expedition to Africa, including food, supplies, and men to carry the tents. When they landed on the African shore, the man contacted the natives to learn about this animal and its whereabouts. Over and over he was told, "You'll never catch one. They're too fast and too strong. You can shoot and kill them from a distance—but you'll never get close enough to take one alive."

He told a reporter who was on the safari with him, "Don't listen to them; I'll get as many of them as I want! And it won't be a problem."

When his men located a herd, he poured sweet feed—a blend of oats and barley rolled in molasses—on the ground in an open area in the middle of the night and left. The next night, he scattered the feed again. For two weeks, he spread the feed, night after night.

The animals, of course, came in and ate it. On the first night of the third week, he scattered the feed and sank an eight-foot post into the ground twenty feet away. The next night, he scattered the feed and sank another post into the ground twenty feet in the opposite direction. Every night, he added a post. Then he started putting boards between the posts while scattering the feed.

Six weeks rolled by. He continued adding posts and boards until he had a corral built around this feed. Every night these animals found the gaps between the posts until, finally, he watched the entire herd squeeze through the final gap. He moved in behind them and nailed the last board into place. The animals were trapped inside the corral.

He chose the animals he wanted to take residency in his zoo and let the others go.

When he was asked how he knew how to catch them, he said something that chills me to the bone: "I treat animals the same way I treat people: I give them what they want. I give them food and shelter. In exchange, they give me their beauty and their freedom."

TRADING FREEDOM

Are you trading your beauty and freedom to help someone else's dreams come true? Way too many people trade out their freedom for security, and they don't even realize it. There is a difference between *an opportunity you seize* and *a trap you walk into*. Being aware of the choice and the trap is the key.

The buck stops here. You're responsible for your past and your future. The bad news is that the past was in your hands, but the good news is that the future is also in your hands.

You trade away your freedom every time you blame your parents, your spouse, your boss, or a colleague for your present situation. You trade away your freedom every time you blame your education (or lack thereof), your genetics, or the circumstantial ebb and flow of everyday life.

THE BAD NEWS IS THAT THE PAST WAS IN
YOUR HANDS, BUT THE GOOD NEWS IS THAT
THE FUTURE IS ALSO IN YOUR HANDS.

If you allow yourself to blame these uncontrollable forces for your lack of success, you forever will be caught in the web of the past, a victim to your fears and frustrations. You cannot let your history control your destiny. By choosing to take responsibility, you can avoid living reactively—selling out your future to circumstances you choose not to control.

You are where you are today—mentally, spiritually, emotionally, financially, and, in many ways, physically—because of decisions you have made. Your decisions have always been governed by your thinking. Therefore, you are where you are today mentally, physically, spiritually, emotionally, and financially because of the quality of your thoughts, the perspectives you have about life, and your beliefs about yourself and others. In other words, your thinking. Do you truly desire a significant change in your life? Change your thinking!

TAKING PERSONAL INVENTORY

To take responsibility for your life, you must first take a personal inventory of where you are right now. In your journal, on a scale from 1 to 10—1 being miserable and 10 outstanding—rate how you feel you're doing in each of the following categories: emotionally, physically, financially, spiritually, socially, professionally, and with your family.

OVERCOMING FEAR OF FAILURE

When a person considers the Responsible Decision, he or she will likely confront the fear of failure. A new realization sets in: *If I'm in control of my life, if I fail, then it really is my fault!*

God did not give you the discernment to make right decisions all the time. He did, however, grant you the ability to make wrong decisions right. Don't allow the rise and fall of your emotional tide to deter you from your course. Your life should not be an apology; it should be a statement—an extraordinary demonstration of the possibilities within all of us.

Another way of looking at failure is to ask yourself how you can use it to catapult your success. Is hitting rock bottom really the signal for your turning point? Although it doesn't feel like it, yes, you bet it is! Why? Great ideas and inspiration often come from rock bottom.

MY MIND WILL NOT DWELL IN THE
PROBLEMS OF THE PAST—IT WILL LIVE
IN THE SOLUTIONS OF THE FUTURE

Thomas Watson, founder of IBM, said, "That's where success lies—on the far side of failure."

When things don't go as planned, it generally means you need to make a course correction. We all have heard how Thomas Edison reportedly responded to the notion that he failed ten thousand times in creating the lightbulb: "I have not failed. I've just found 10,000 ways that won't work."

When you view your failures as opportunities for growth and discovery, you free yourself from the fear of failure. How can you fail when your failures are merely lessons you learned on your way to success?

LEARNING FROM FAILURE

What has been your biggest failure so far in your life's adventure?

Think about it. What came out of that experience? What did you learn? How is your life now different or better as a consequence of this "failure"?

Write down in your journal what you learned from this failure.

OG'S INITIATIVE FOR SUCCESS

I want to tell you the story of a man whose failures took him to the brink of destruction and back, paving the way for massive success. You may recognize the name Og Mandino even though he passed away in 1996. His seventeen books still grace the shelves of most bookstores in America. This man was an incredible influence on my life although I wasn't acquainted with him personally.

Og Mandino was told by his mother—his champion and cheerleader—that he could be a successful writer. She died before he went to college. Aimlessly, Og joined the army after high school and fought in World War II. (He was a bombardier in the same squadron as Jimmy Stewart.)

Og returned to the United States after the war and discovered there wasn't much employment for bombardiers with only a high school education. The next ten years of his life were a living hell for him, his wife, and their daughter. He struggled to sell insurance, and it seemed that no matter how much he worked, his young family drifted deeper and deeper into debt.

Like so many frustrated individuals, he responded by hiding from his problems. After a long day of sales calls, he would stop by the bar and get a drink. One drink turned into two, two turned into three, and three into six. Eventually when his wife and daughter could no longer endure his behavior or his words, they left him. The following two years of his life were a blur. He traveled the country in an old Ford, doing odd jobs to earn enough money for another bottle of wine. He spent countless nights in the gutter, literally—"a sorry wretch of a human being," as he put it.

One cold winter morning in Cleveland, he almost took his life. He paused at the window of a dingy pawnshop, gazing inside at a small handgun with a yellow tag attached: $29. He reached in his pocket and pulled out three ten-dollar bills. *I could afford a couple of bullets. I'll go back to that room where I'm staying, and I'll never have to look at myself in the mirror again.*

For whatever reason, Og did not kill himself. Years later he joked about it, saying he was such a spineless person at the time, he couldn't muster the courage! As the snow fell that day in Cleveland, he turned from the pawnshop and wandered to a public library.

IN THE FUTURE, WHEN I AM TEMPTED TO ASK
THE QUESTION "WHY ME?" I WILL IMMEDIATELY
COUNTER WITH THE ANSWER, "WHY *NOT* ME?"
CHALLENGES ARE GIFTS, OPPORTUNITIES TO
LEARN. PROBLEMS ARE THE COMMON THREAD
RUNNING THROUGH THE LIVES OF GREAT
MEN AND WOMEN. IN TIMES OF ADVERSITY,
I WILL NOT HAVE A PROBLEM TO DEAL
WITH; I WILL HAVE A CHOICE TO MAKE.

Og entered the self-help section and began to read fervently. For several months he spent almost every afternoon and evening in the library, reading book after book until he found one called *Success Through a Positive Mental Attitude*, by W. Clement Stone, the chairman and founder of Combined Insurance of America. He was so impressed by the idea that he could think his way to a different future that he began to apply the principles to every part of his life.

After becoming a successful insurance salesman for W. Clement Stone, he did what his mother had always wanted him to do—and what he had always wanted to do too—he became a writer for Stone's company's young magazine, *Success Unlimited*. He eventually became the editor of *Success Unlimited* and grew it from an in-house publication to a national publication with 250,000 subscribers.

One day, several months after he became the magazine's editor, he was short one article, with only a few days until press time. There was nothing suitable in the files. Since Og was a golf nut, he worked all night on a piece about golfer Ben Hogan, who had gone from being nearly left in a wheelchair after a terrible automobile accident to winning the U.S. Open.

Og ran the article in *Success Unlimited*, and several weeks later he received a letter from a New York publisher who had enjoyed the Hogan article. He offered Og the opportunity to submit a manuscript for review by the publishing house. Believe me, as an author, this is the kind of letter we dream about receiving!

Eighteen months after receiving that letter, Og's first book, *The Greatest Salesman in the World*, was published. When my mom and dad passed away, and I ended up sleeping under the pier, my own life at a total dead end, it was that book along with its little corollary, *The Greatest Secret in the World*, that I read over and over again.

It is absolutely amazing to see what has happened since that book's first printing of 5,000 copies. Soon total sales reached 350,000, and then 500,000. Since his death in 1996, the book has continued to sell, with more than 50 million copies of Og Mandino's books sold worldwide.

Most of Og's writings were about people in tough situations who overcame their problems and achieved extraordinary success. His failures became his inspiration for helping other men and women hang in there until the tide turned. Og Mandino has been gone for years now, but because he was willing to build on his failure, his legacy lives on, and he continues to inspire millions of people.

THE EFFECT OF OUR DECISIONS

To fully understand that you are where you are as a result of your decisions, do the following:

Choose an area of your life from the Taking Personal Inventory exercise on page 10.

1. Reflect on the choices you have made in the past that may have contributed to your current situation. If you chose finances, consider the decisions that contributed to your current financial situation. For example, perhaps you had the choice of starting a business or staying in your current job. Or maybe you could have contributed more to your IRA or pension plan. The purpose of this exercise isn't to make you feel bad for past decisions but to trace your decisions to where you are right now. Remember, every decision *not* to do something is still a decision.
2. List at least five decisions (big or small) you have made or didn't make over the last five years that have contributed to where you are in that area of your life.

> Do you notice any pattern? Are you beginning to see
> how you have greater power to influence your results
> than you may have previously realized?

A DEFEATED WASHINGTON

It has been more than two hundred years since George Washington
walked among the admiring patriots of early America. Commander-
in-chief of the Continental Army during the American Revolution
and the first president of the United States, Washington left a
legacy ingrained into the fabric of our country for over two centuries. Interestingly, Washington never wanted to be president; he
treasured his private life with his wife, Martha. His willingness to
sacrifice his own desires for future generations laid the foundation
on which the American dream was birthed.

Washington's courage, determination, and character, and especially his sense of responsibility, inspired his countrymen. He
consistently made the Responsible Decision.

The complex task of establishing a nation was wrought with
challenges and missteps for Washington. Fortunately, the mistakes
he made in his latter years bore little resemblance to the grave blun-
ders the father of our country made during the dawn of his military
career. These lessons cost many brave and honorable men under
his command their lives, and nearly resulted in his own demise. As
providence would have it, Washington was able to accept responsibility, learn from his missteps, and turn his early defeats into what
we see today as a victorious life.

In 1754, as a young major in the Virginia militia, Washington was
ordered to lead 350 raw recruits through the wilderness to French-
occupied Fort Duquesne at present-day Pittsburgh. Traveling four

miles per day, the militia camped at a spot some forty miles from Fort Duquesne and erected a fort named Necessity.

They advanced on the enemy until seven hundred French soldiers and their Indian allies clashed with Washington and his men, driving them back into Fort Necessity. The fort didn't live up to its name. Its location made it impossible to defend because it was surrounded by hills that were the perfect hiding place from which French and Indian fighters could attack. The enemy took its time, firing on Washington and his men from behind rocks and trees. Many of Washington's men were drunk, and the casualties began to mount. In nine short hours, with thirty dead, seventy wounded, and many more deserting, the battle was over.

Defeated, Washington was forced to give over his sword and sign hastily drafted articles of surrender by candlelight in a driving rainstorm. George Washington, the future "father of our country," lost his first battle, his first fort, and his first command in one fell swoop. Because of this humiliating defeat, the French controlled the entire Ohio Valley, and Indians freely attacked settlers all along the frontier.

As Washington limped back to Virginia to his beloved Mount Vernon, he resolved to learn from this miserable failure. He made no excuses. No "Well, they had more men than we did," or "Well, my men were drunk and not as skilled." Instead, Washington learned to use the guerrilla warfare strategies of the Indians.

During the American Revolution, Washington remembered his earlier lessons at the Battles of Trenton and King's Mountain. The settlers attacked the proud British forces from the cover of rocks and trees, routing them and humiliating them before achieving total victory for the new nation.

When we take responsibility, we realize that failure can be a classroom for the most profound lessons for success.

CRAFTING YOUR ULTIMATE VISION

Many people complain about where they are in life; however, very few people know where they want to be. In the Taking Personal Inventory exercise on page 10, you rated each major area of your life from 1 to 10. Do you know what a 10 would look like for you?

As you've heard before, if you don't know where you're going, it's quite challenging to get there. Or as Yogi Berra put it, "If you don't know where you're going, you'll end up someplace else."

Think about the overall lifestyle you want to create, and craft the Ultimate Vision for your life—what it will look like when it's a 10. Here are a few questions to consider:

1. What will your relationships be like—within your family, socially, and professionally?
2. What will your finances look like? What will your business affairs look like?
3. What will your overall emotional patterns look like? Will you be a master of your emotions? How will you know when you're *truly* happy?
4. In what areas of your life will you grow the most? What will you attract into your life as a consequence of your growth?
5. How will you handle yourself in difficult situations?
6. How will you grow spiritually?

EMBRACING THE GIFT OF ADVERSITY

Back in the day when I was reading all of those biographies, besides discovering seven common denominators, I realized an additional factor found in every single case: each person had to battle *adversity*. In fact, problems seemed to be a common experience of great people throughout time.

That's right: the stories of wealthy, influential, successful world-changers are constantly riddled with adversity. Each one was presented with the challenge of accepting responsibility for his or her decisions and circumstances—and each one did. But I'm sure they were tempted to play the victim, as most of us are, and ask, *Why me?*

When my parents died and I ran out of money—when things went from bad to worse—my constant refrain was, *Why me? Why is this happening to me?* I woke with *Why me?* I went to bed with *Why me?* I walked around all day long thinking, *Why me?*

NEVER AGAIN WILL I BLAME MY PAST FOR MY PRESENT CONDITION. I WILL LOOK FORWARD. I WILL NOT LET MY HISTORY CONTROL MY DESTINY.

My life began to change when I understood that adversity is a common experience of great people. Instead of feeling sorry for myself, I began to get excited. I realized that adversity is more like a toll bridge than an insurmountable roadblock on the way to success. My problems became less invasive—I no longer felt as though they were *always* going to be there. Unfortunately, many people run from their problems, not realizing that they are necessary stops on the road to the life they want.

I began to wonder, *Is adversity what helps people become great?* Overcoming adversity strengthened my problem-solving skills, and demonstrating a positive response to adversity magnetically drew people to me.

Adversity prepares you for greatness. Challenges are gifts. Problems present opportunities to learn and grow. In times of adversity, you don't have a problem to deal with; you have a choice to make.

Why you?

Why *not* you?!

Why shouldn't you be prepared for something great?

REALIZING YOUR FUTURE IDENTITY

Now that you have identified your Ultimate Vision, ask yourself, *Who do I need to become to realize this vision?* Albert Einstein said, "A problem cannot be solved by the same consciousness that created it." Like it or not, you are where you are because of *what you are* right now. As a human spirit with enormous potential, you are bound only by your self-imposed limitations.

Review your Ultimate Vision. Answer the question, "Who do I need to become to realize this vision?"

How will you need to treat other people? How will you need to treat yourself? What will you need to read and study? What lessons will you need to learn? With whom will you need to surround yourself? What will you need to think and believe about yourself? What will you need to believe about those around you?

Capture as many ideas as you can in your journal.

REAL TRAVELER PROFILE: JIMMY DEAN

I first met Jimmy Dean at a Nashville television studio, where we were taping a show. I always enjoyed talking with him—I loved his good humor, and he told some of the best jokes I have ever heard!

In 1928, Mr. Dean was born into poverty on a farm in Plainview, Texas. He began his musical career performing in nightclubs and on the radio. In the '60s, he became a nationally known personality through his popular television shows on CBS and ABC, and he was Johnny Carson's first guest host on *The Tonight Show*. His Grammy-winning country music album *Big Bad John* sold more than six million copies. Ironically, it was a benefit at which he performed for a faded country music star that led Jimmy Dean to a career change that took him to even greater financial success. Jimmy told me that he left the concert that night thinking, *By gosh, no one is ever going to have to do a benefit for Jimmy Dean!*

Within the year, Jimmy diversified from the entertainment world, launching a successful food line including the most popular sausage in the country. In 1985, Jimmy Dean Foods merged with the Sara Lee Corporation to achieve combined annual sales exceeding a half billion dollars. He was inducted into the Texas Country Music Hall of Fame in 2005, and an exhibit of his life is on display at the Texas Country Music Museum in Carthage, Texas.

Read how Jimmy Dean personifies the Responsible Decision.

Dear Andy:

In your letter, you addressed my "success and wealth." To me, success and wealth have always been a state of mind. My grandfather, W. J. Taylor, was the most successful and wealthy man I ever knew, and I doubt seriously that he ever made more than $10,000 in any given year in his life. But he was the best farmer in Hale County, Texas. He knew that. He had the straightest fences, the cleanest end-rows. He had the neatest barn and the neatest house. He raised nine kids; he had a great relationship with the man upstairs and a wonderful inner peace. To me, this is success and wealth.

Many look at me and say, "He's the luckiest S.O.B. that ever lived." It is true—I have had much good fortune, but things were not—and are not—always easy. I have probably had almost as many rejections as acceptances, but I have ascertained that, were it not for the rough roads, you would never appreciate the super highways.

Being knocked down is part of life—getting up is also part of life, and I have very little use for people who cannot bounce back from the bludgeoning of temporary setbacks. Being able to handle temporary setbacks (notice I did not say defeat—the word *defeat* is not in my vocabulary), overcome them, and stand tall is what entitles you to the sweet bows of victory.

We, unfortunately, in this wonderful country have created an element that condones giving up. In my opinion, when our great president, F.D.R., decided it was proper that we compensate people for nonproductivity, it was the gravest mistake that ever happened.

The good book says, "You'll earn your bread by the sweat of your brow," as it should be. I have no use for anyone who can help himself and does not. Reminds me of once when I told my youngest son, Robert, that I was a self-made man, and he said, "That's what I like about you, Dad, you take the blame for everything." It's just that this country has been so wonderful to me, I would like it to remain the land of opportunity for my great, great grandkids.

I feel, instead of every day creating another organization for the weak, we should create organizations that make people want to stand on their own two feet and say, "I believe in me." We cannot create a muddle of mediocrity that makes people feel the world owes them a living.

Every time I talk like this, someone will invariably say, "Easy for you to talk like that; God gave you talent." Damn right he gave me talent; he gave everyone a talent. My greatest fear is that with all our federal aid, state aid, city aid, county aids, etc. that they're going to be many wonderfully talented people who will never be forced to find out what their talents are.

Sincerely yours,

Jimmy Dean
JD:BMM

TWO

THE GUIDED DECISION

I WILL SEEK WISDOM.

God moves mountains to create the opportunity of His choosing. It is up to you to be ready to move yourself.

Your past cannot be changed, but you will change your future by changing your actions today. The Guided Decision teaches us to actively seek wisdom to help us craft lives of extraordinary achievement.

I WILL SEEK WISDOM.

Knowing that wisdom waits to be gathered, I will actively search her out. My past can never be changed, but I can change the future by changing my actions today. I *will* change my actions today! I will train my eyes and ears to read and listen to books and recordings that bring about positive changes in my personal relationships and a greater understanding of my fellow man. No longer will I bombard my mind with materials that feed my doubts and fears. I will read and listen only to that which increases my belief in myself and my future.

I will seek wisdom. I will choose my friends with care.

I am who my friends are. I speak their language, and I wear their clothes. I share their opinions and habits. From this moment forward, I will choose to associate with people whose lives and lifestyles I admire. If I associate with chickens, I will learn to scratch at the ground and squabble over crumbs. If I associate with eagles, I will learn to soar great heights. I am an eagle. It is my destiny to fly.

I will seek wisdom. I will listen to the counsel of wise men.

The words of a wise man are like raindrops on dry ground. They are precious and quickly used for immediate results. Only the blade of grass that catches a raindrop will prosper and grow. The person who ignores wise counsel is like the blade of grass untouched by the rain—soon to wither and die. When I counsel with myself, I can only make decisions according to what I already know. By counseling with a wise man, I add his knowledge and experience to my own and dramatically increase my success.

I will seek wisdom. I will be a servant to others.

A wise man will cultivate a servant's spirit, for that particular attribute attracts people like no other. As I humbly serve others, their wisdom will be freely shared with me. Often, the person who develops a servant's spirit becomes wealthy beyond measure. Many times, a servant has the ear of the king, and a humble servant becomes king, for he is the popular choice of the people. He who serves the most grows the fastest.

I will become a humble servant. I will not look for someone to open my door—I will look to open the door for someone. I will not be distressed when no one is available to help me—I will be excited when I am available to help.

I will be a servant to others. I will listen to the counsel of wise men. I will choose my friends with care.

I will seek wisdom.

SEEKING WISDOM

Most people mistake wisdom for education, like a high school diploma or college degree. Seeking wisdom is not the same as gaining knowledge: Knowledge is a precursor to wisdom. Wisdom includes an intuitive element, an insight gained from personal experience that serves us as we make choices in our lives. Seeking wisdom should be a continual process. The humility of the wisdom seeker is a defining characteristic of influential, wealthy, successful people.

Wisdom is available to all, waiting to be known. It can't be bartered or sold; wisdom is a gift only for the diligent, because only the diligent can find it. The lazy person doesn't look in the first place.

God moves mountains to create the opportunity of His choosing, but it's up to you to be ready to move yourself.

There are three simple things you can do daily to chart your lifelong search for wisdom: read, take the counsel of others, and *serve others*. They may seem obvious, yet tragically, much of our society has ignored these simple, critical distinctions despite their availability.

WORDS OF WISDOM

First, read.

I know—you're thinking, *Read? That's it?*

Yes. Read.

Read books. Magazines, newspapers, and social media inform and entertain, but wisdom is generally not found there.

We're encouraged to read books as children, but as adults, we've forgotten this vital piece of advice. What do you call a child who reads two books a year? *Slow.* What do you call an adult who reads two books a year? *Normal.* Amazingly, the national average for books read by American adults is *less than two books a year.*

You wouldn't believe how many times I've had people brag to me, "I determined when I got out of college that I would never read another book again. And I have been true to my word. I read magazines and newspapers, but I've never read another book. I haven't read a book in twenty years."

And they're proud of it! I smile, nod, and sadly think to myself, *They are not on the path for my personal search for wisdom.* These are not folks with whom I can afford to become close. Their search for wisdom ended years ago.

You, my friend, obviously already know that few things affect you like time alone with a good book, highlighter in hand. And the highlighter or pen is critical. We're not sitting with the book in our hands, passively waiting for some profound words of wisdom to leap from the page; rather, we're *actively* seeking wisdom. Even now, as you read these words, be on the lookout for something that will *change everything*. One idea has the power to transform your life forever, but you must first recognize it.

THE PAST WILL NEVER CHANGE, BUT YOU
CAN CHANGE THE FUTURE BY CHANGING
YOUR ACTIONS TODAY. IT IS REALLY A
VERY SIMPLE PROCESS. WE, AS HUMANS,
ARE ALWAYS IN A PROCESS OF CHANGE.
THEREFORE, WE MIGHT AS WELL GUIDE THE
DIRECTION IN WHICH WE WILL CHANGE.

If you don't think you can take the time to read, you can always listen to audiobooks. Whenever I say something like this at a seminar, people often tell me, "You don't know what my life is like. I have a job. My wife has a job. I have kids. I'm the president of the social club. You're telling me you want me to read books and listen to recordings?"

People think they have to clear the house and their calendar, sit down at the table with a pen and paper, and stare at the wall with their headphones on while they take notes. You don't have to pay attention like that. All you have to do is press the play button. Listen while you're cooking, mowing the lawn, or driving the kids to school. Listen while you're in the shower. Listen while you're sleeping. You'll get it. After all, consider the number of commercial jingles or television show theme songs you have inadvertently memorized. If anything is going to be programming your subconscious mind, why not *choose* the programming? Why not choose something that can change your family's future for generations?

There are many choices, with literally millions of books and audio programs that can be purchased on the Internet or through your local bookstore. In addition, your local library is a treasure trove just waiting to be discovered. To find your next treasure, discuss your interests with a friend you admire, find out what has done well in the marketplace, or read reviews on online bookstores. Oftentimes, I find out about a great book because it's referenced in another book I'm reading, as if I'm led from one book to the next in a continual strand of wisdom.

If you're looking for something on leadership, you might want to check out John Maxwell. My favorite of his works is *21 Irrefutable Laws of Leadership*. Og Mandino wrote a library during his lifetime that has changed the lives of millions of people. *The Greatest Secret in the World* changed my life. I read that book at least four hundred times. People have often commented, "You gotta be kidding me. A book? You read a book four hundred times? I mean, what is it you didn't understand?!"

I'm not reading just to read, to add to my gun belt of books read. I am reading on a search for wisdom. If you desire wisdom, read.

CONSTRUCTING YOUR PERSONAL LIBRARY

Wisdom in the words of successful men and women throughout history can be found in books. You are who you spend time with, and you are what you read. There's nothing wrong with reading magazines for entertainment, but wisdom is generally found in nonfiction books or fiction with a specific point or purpose.

Oftentimes, we "accidentally" get conditioned into reading only nonfiction books that are related to our primary field of interest (i.e., what we do for a living). Sometimes it's useful to explore subjects that seem to have nothing to do with your occupational endeavors and let your mind make its own connections.

For example, perhaps you've always been interested in studying creativity, painting, aquatic life, theoretical biology, quantum mechanics, sewing, basket weaving, gardening, personal finances, branding, real estate, architecture, leadership, sales, or consciousness research. Any topic can prove useful if you're open and ready to receive the connections.

In your journal list ten subjects you've always been curious about. Within the next twenty-four hours, go online or visit your local bookstore or library to pick up a few titles that spark your interest.

The Power of Fellowship

As humans, we're always changing. The past doesn't change, but you can change your future by changing your actions today. Change is inevitable, so we might as well guide the direction in which we change.

So how can you guide the direction of your change? Besides reading, you must choose your companions wisely.

We all know how important the right peer group is for kids. Most parents are desperately concerned about the friends with whom their own children hang out—we understand that our kids are likely to turn out just like those friends. If our children's companions are doing drugs, having sex, or using profane language, our kids are obviously at a greater risk for exhibiting similar behaviors.

We're concerned about our children's choice of companions, and yet we ignore this principle as adults. At what age does this principle cease to work in someone's life? Do we become immune to the influence of others at age eighteen? Twenty-one? Or maybe it's no longer a factor at age thirty-five or forty?

You know the answer: it's always a factor. If you are surrounded by people who use bad language, your language will tend toward that. If you hang around people with certain viewpoints, you will be persuaded by those views. If you spend time with people who are lazy, you will tend toward laziness. If you are comfortable with people who make excuses, you will tend to make excuses as well.

GUARD YOUR ASSOCIATIONS CAREFULLY.
ANYTIME YOU TOLERATE MEDIOCRITY IN
YOUR CHOICE OF COMPANIONS, YOU BECOME
MORE COMFORTABLE WITH MEDIOCRITY IN
YOUR OWN LIFE. IF A LAZY MAN ISN'T AN
IRRITATION TO YOU, IT'S A SIGN THAT YOU HAVE
ACCEPTED SLOTHFULNESS AS A WAY OF LIFE.

When you tolerate mediocrity in your choice of companions, you're going to become more accepting of mediocrity in your own life. Here's something to consider: if a lazy person isn't an irritation to you, it's a sign you've accepted laziness as "normal" in your own life.

It's critical to choose your friends with care. I often ask people, "What is a true friend to you?"

More than 80 percent of the time, I hear, "A true friend is someone who accepts me as I am."

My friend, this is dangerous garbage to believe. *A true friend is someone who accepts you as you are?* The kid who works the drive-thru at your local fast-food restaurant accepts you as you are—because he doesn't care anything about you. A true friend holds you to a higher standard—he or she expects you to do what you said you were going to do, when you said you were going to do it. A true friend makes you better by his or her presence.

When you were growing up, do you remember playing tennis or Ping-Pong with your father? I'm betting he didn't let you win all of the time, because he knew if he did, you wouldn't get any better. This works with the companions you choose too. Choose allies who are better than you. If you want to get better at tennis, play somebody who will beat you, because it improves your game.

This concept works in business too. Surround yourself with people who are better than you. Want to become wealthier? Spend time with people who are wealthier than you. Want to become wiser? Invest time with people who have wisdom in spades. And seek their counsel.

For a great deal of my life, I hung out with a quiet guy who didn't talk until somebody asked him a question. When I understood the principle of seeking wisdom, his way of being became clear to me: My friend had an abundance of wisdom, but you had to draw it out of him. He wasn't keeping it from anybody, but he was humble. I really had to hammer him with questions. *Why this? Why that?* Only a fool refuses the counsel of wise men. As a businessperson, as a parent, as a student, there is safety in wise counsel.

A friend of mine had a history of bad decisions. I would ask him, "Now, just out of curiosity, who did you talk to about this before you made that decision?"

He would look at me like I was out of my mind and say, "Well, nobody."

And I'd reply, "So, you didn't ask anybody? You just . . . kind of . . . decided?"

He gave me a familiar look and basically said, "I'm an adult, and I know what's best for me. I can make my own decisions."

When we take counsel from ourselves, all we can receive is what we have . . . what we know . . . what we are.

Taking the counsel of wise men and women helps us avoid bad decisions and puts us on the pathway to a more successful life. When we add someone's wisdom to our own, we greatly increase the probability of our success.

HARNESSING YOUR INNER CIRCLE

The Guided Decision teaches us that, to a large degree, we are who we spend time with.

1. In your journal list everyone you consider to be in your "inner circle"—those closest to you who influence your life, including family members, friends, and colleagues.

2. The Guided Decision teaches us that our peers either stretch us or burden us. Next to each name, put an arrow to denote which direction the person is leading you. (This can be a difficult exercise for many of us because we form attachments to even those "friends"

---

who hinder our progress. Be honest as you evaluate
who you spend time with.)

3. Do you see any patterns? Are there a few people with
whom you spend time who generally sour your life
experiences? Or do you invest most of your time
with those souls who challenge you, uplift you, and
help you to become more?

YOUR BOARD OF DIRECTORS

I personally don't make any decisions on my own without counsel from others I respect. And post-living-under-the-pier, I have a
pretty good track record of good decisions. Logically, wouldn't
you be more likely to make good decisions if you're surrounded
with high-level thinking from others? I leverage the insights, experiences, and decision-making abilities of intelligent people—and
select three or four to be on my personal board of directors to help
me make decisions. What are the chances I'm going to screw up
big-time when I have the counsel of wise people in my life? Find
people you can rely on and from whom you can seek counsel. This
is a critical component of seeking wisdom!

The acquisition of wisdom is greatly expedited by harness-
ing the wisdom of others. People sometimes think, *I don't have
the money to hire a board of directors. That's too expensive!* They miss
the point. The idea is to surround yourself with wise people. My
"board members" don't actually know they're on my board of
directors. I don't necessarily let them know they're influencing my
decision making.

It's easy to create a personal board; simply find people who are smarter than you, are more skilled than you, and have more fruit on the tree in key parts of their life.

My wife, Polly, and I have several couples on our board of directors who have been married longer than us. Polly and I have been married almost twenty years, and both of these couples have been married more than thirty-five years. For more than three decades, they have been happy and loyal to each other. I look at them and wonder, *How have they done it?* Naturally, we want them on our board of directors.

Polly and I do the same thing with people who have already raised the kind of children we want to raise. I stock my personal board of directors with people who are wiser, better writers, healthier—those who have created for their families the life I want for mine.

CREATING YOUR BOARD OF DIRECTORS

With whom might you cultivate a relationship (or make better use of an existing one) to create your own personal board of directors? You may choose specific advisers for various areas of your life. Naturally, you wouldn't want a health adviser who smokes or sits around all day watching television. We must become masters at knowing where to seek the appropriate counsel.

In your journal, list the names of potential board members and the area of your life in which they would advise you. Don't limit yourself to the people in your inner circle; brainstorm who you'd love to have on your board of directors, even if you don't currently have a relationship with him or her.

Remember, you don't even have to tell these people they're on your board—it can be your own little secret. And sometimes, the information you receive will be more to the point and pure without your directors being aware of the pressure of mentoring.

BEWARE OF THE DANGER POINT

When we reach a certain level of success with these Seven Decisions, it is also typical to come upon a danger point. We must always remember: we are where we are because of our best thinking, and if we want to keep improving, we must transcend that level of thinking, whether we intuitively know where to improve or are receiving good counsel from our inner circle of friends. It gets dangerous when, following an abundance of success, we begin to think, *I have it covered. It's wired. It's done. I understand. And now I'm free to make all the decisions myself.* Our actions begin to say, *I'm wiser and smarter than anyone else.*

As you become more successful, you'll find the path less traveled. There will be fewer people available to you who are stronger and wiser than you; but you can find them. Of course, you can benefit from almost everyone if you're a committed student of wisdom. Somebody doesn't have to be wealthier than you to be smarter than you. Everybody is superior to us in some or many ways—we can learn from anyone.

GOD MOVES MOUNTAINS TO CREATE THE
OPPORTUNITY OF HIS CHOOSING, BUT IT'S UP
TO YOU TO BE READY TO MOVE YOURSELF.

The danger point occurs when we begin to think too highly of our own wisdom and start ignoring the counsel of others. Remember Napoleon? He went down in history as an emperor, a leader of men, and someone who conquered what was considered the world at that time. But here's the story most people have never heard . . .

AN AFTERNOON IN WATERLOO

In June 1815, Napoleon was about to defeat Wellington at Waterloo and, in fact, *did so*. (In *The Hinge Factor* Erik Durschmied lays out a detailed sketch of the Battle of Waterloo and outlines how Napoleon defeated Wellington. If you really want to understand how Napoleon pulled off this incredible feat, I highly recommend this book.)

In February 1815, Napoleon fled from Elba, where he had been exiled by the Allied governments, signaling the start of what they called the "100 Days Campaign." During this time, nobody slept well in the capitals of Europe for fear of Napoleon. Once Napoleon reached Paris, he organized an army to sweep across Europe. His old generals were either dead or had switched allegiance. Davout had been killed at Marengo; LaNey at Esperge; Janeaux shot himself. It didn't matter to Napoleon because he believed he was capable of independent command. He was a military genius. After all, everyone told him so.

Just after daylight, Napoleon was having breakfast with his generals at the emperor's headquarters at Roson Farm. One of the generals worried about Wellington's strong position, being situated at Monte St. John. The emperor scoffed, "We have no possibility of defeat!" And, of course, he didn't! Napoleon had 72,000 men and 246 cannons compared to Wellington's 67,000 men and 156 guns.

Napoleon rode a small gray horse and was dressed in a gray topcoat with a dark purple silk vest and white trousers over boots that came just past his knees. As he was about to send his troops into battle, the emperor turned to his general, Michael Ney, and said, "If my orders are well executed, we shall sleep tonight in Brussels." All day long Napoleon sent wave after wave of infantry into Wellington's forces. At the end of the afternoon, General Ney and the Fourth Corps of Cavalry—his greatest group of five thousand riders—were ready. The sun shimmered off five thousand swords and lance tips, pennants fluttering in the wind as the emperor reviewed the situation one last time. One bold sweep, he knew, would separate the enemy from their guns. Then, he would cut them down. *Yes, it would work.* A well-executed cavalry attack was more devastating than the actual losses sustained by the enemy. Because of this, he would not divide his divisions; rather, he would attack in a single broad front. It was 4:03 p.m.

The French Cavalry advanced in echelon, supported by the artillery. The division was in the center of the attack. The emperor's riders headed directly for the British batteries. And when the British guns opened up with their double-shotted canister, thousands of round pellets fired as Ney pointed his saber forward to signal *La Charge!*

Five thousand horses broke into full gallop, the ground trembling from the pounding of hooves. *"Vive L'Empereur!"*

On the other side, Colonel Cornelius Frazier, battalion commander for Wellington, saw an unbelievable sight: a steel tide advancing on his position! *They'll roll right over us!* he panicked. How many rounds could his gunners loosen off? Napoleon's men, led by General Ney, riding two ranks deep, knee to knee, headed straight for Cornelius Frazier's deadly balls of fire.

Wellington's canisters tore into limbs and turned horses inside out. Riders went down, but nothing stopped the charge. At the sound of the bugle, five thousand spear tips appeared in front of their horses to form a battering ram of pointed steel.

Another blast from the enemy's guns tore into the line of riders. Every gun, every battery on the hill, was blasting away, but nothing stopped the heroic charge of these five thousand men of the Fourth Cavalry.

The gunners managed to loosen off one more round of canisters as riders and horses piled up on each other like cards. Five minutes into the battle, General Ney was out in front, watching gunners drop their sponge-staves and flee their cannons. His men ran over them and captured the cannons. They had driven the English from their artillery, they had captured their guns, and Napoleon had defeated Wellington at Waterloo.

NAPOLEON'S BLUNDER

It's a great story, isn't it? And it's absolutely true. *Now, wait a minute!* you must be thinking. *I thought Napoleon lost at Waterloo!* Well . . . he did lose. But first, he won. You just never hear about the win because the loss overshadowed everything else.

Consider the situation: Here's a guy who's achieved so much success that he's not listening to anybody, not even his generals, much less the colonels, sergeants, or privates. He's so obsessed with his idea of victory that he refuses counsel from anybody.

And now for the blunder: Both the French and the English artillery carried muzzle-loading, bronze, twelve-to-sixteen-pound cannons, fired by setting a glowing fuse or a machete to a narrow firing touchhole that was drilled through the solid bronze. When troops would overrun an opponent's cannon, they took headless nails and drove them down into that touchhole, rendering the cannon useless. Napoleon's troops had asked before the battle, "Where are the nails? We're about to go into battle without nails!" Their confusion was ignored.

Napoleon's men were on the battlefield with no nails. They had guns, horses, swords, lances, and artillery pieces, but no nails. This historic event was decided by a fistful of nails.

Napoleon absolutely defeated Wellington. He ran Wellington over. But the battle raged back and forth, until finally a group of Wellington's men got their cannons back, and then another group . . . Suddenly, the cannons were being turned back upon Napoleon's force, firing into them, and Napoleon had to stand there on the hill with his hands behind his back, watching his men who had defeated Wellington's forces be blasted to pieces—all because they didn't bring nails into the battle. A handful of nails would have put those cannons out of action, and history books today would contain the record of Wellington's defeat.

When you counsel with only yourself, you make decisions only according to what you know. By counseling with wise men and women, you add their knowledge and experience to your own, dramatically increasing your chances for success and decreasing the possibility of failure.

LEARNING TO SERVE OTHERS

In addition to reading books and taking the counsel of wiser friends, the third way to chart a course toward wisdom is by serving others—find a way to help another human being. This doesn't mean you have to do something grandiose or even something you consider incredibly useful. Serving others could be opening the door for someone. Carry their luggage, pour their coffee, hold their chair. By serving others, we value them, and this increases our own value.

Perhaps not coincidentally, when we serve others, we increase the possibility that they would share their wisdom with us. When billionaire and shipping tycoon Aristotle Onassis was in his last years, a reporter asked, "If you lost all your money, what would you do to gain it back?"

He replied, "Well, it would be a process, of course. But the first step on the process of gaining a fortune, I would consider, to be serving others."

The reporter just dropped his jaw and exclaimed, "What do you mean, *serving others*? I thought people served you!"

A WISE MAN WILL CULTIVATE A SERVANT'S
SPIRIT, FOR THAT PARTICULAR ATTRIBUTE
ATTRACTS PEOPLE LIKE NO OTHER.

He said, "People serve me, but it is only because throughout my life, I've served others. You ask, 'How would you create a fortune?' and the first step would be to serve others. I would put myself in a position, by serving others, to be around people who could help me, guide me, and share their wisdom and experience with me."

Then he added: "I would get a job, maybe two, maybe three. I would save my money. I would live as simply as I possibly could, and when I'd saved up five hundred dollars, I'd go eat in a restaurant that cost five hundred dollars for a meal. Then I would work more, live simply, and save my money until I saved five hundred dollars, and I would go eat again in a restaurant that costs five hundred dollars."

The reporter was beside himself at this point, and replied, "I'm really not getting this. You're trying to create a fortune, yet you're blowing five hundred dollars on a dinner?"

Onassis replied, "It has nothing to do with the food I eat, but the associations that I create. You see, to get to where I'd want to be, I would need the wisdom and relationships with the people who eat regularly in expensive restaurants. And so, when I go into the restaurant, I make eye contact, I introduce myself, I shake hands. As I enter, I say, 'Hello.' As I leave, I say, 'Good-bye.' Somewhere down the road, I'm going to run into those people, who will say, 'Oh, yes, I saw you in . . .' Or 'You were the man at the next table when we ate at . . .'"

He concluded, "It all has to do with the associations you create with the people whom you are around. People will want to help because you were there to hold a chair or hold a door for them."

ALFRED VANDERBILT'S SERVANT SPIRIT

Alfred Vanderbilt was recognized everywhere he went. The Vanderbilt family was one of the wealthiest, most prominent families in the world. The family's wealth began with Alfred's father, Cornelius Vanderbilt, who in the early nineteenth century began amassing a fortune in the shipping and railroad industries.

Alfred stood out among his siblings. He was the only one in the family who insisted on beginning his business experience at the bottom as a clerk in one of his father's offices. His siblings demanded management positions. The public respected Alfred Vanderbilt and never forgot him. His father never forgot him either, as evidenced by the division of his father's wealth: each of Cornelius's sons and daughters was willed $7 million, but Alfred received $76 million. In his father's view, Alfred would steward the money with a servant's spirit. Cornelius Vanderbilt knew that servants often become kings and, consequently, the wealthiest among us.

Alfred Vanderbilt shared his wealth with a servant's spirit. During World War I, Alfred wasn't content with charity in the form of purchasing wagons and giving them to the Red Cross—he intended to drive them himself. He was known as a kind man, known for his kind heart to the poor.

Alfred Vanderbilt's legacy was as a servant (his story is an integral part of my second novel, *The Lost Choice*). His actions during his life's final moments aboard the RMS *Lusitania* testified to his servant's spirit. When the *Lusitania* sank in May 1915, the newspapers memorialized Alfred's servant's spirit: his last act on earth was to tie life jackets to baskets for babies, and he gave his own life jacket to a woman. Though Alfred owned many estates with swimming pools, he had never learned to swim. Alfred Vanderbilt maintained a servant's spirit to the very end.

CULTIVATING THE SERVANT'S SPIRIT

What can you do to begin or continue cultivating a servant's spirit? Can you volunteer at your local church or community center? Can you visit the elderly at your local hospital?

Can you spend more time with your family? Can you schedule a call to a family member just to make him or her smile? Can you commit random acts of kindness, such as paying the toll for the car behind you?

Brainstorm a list of ideas, and commit to doing at least one in the next five days.

FULLER'S LIFE EXPERIMENT

In 1927, at age thirty-two, Buckminster Fuller stood on the shores of Lake Michigan, intent on committing suicide by throwing himself into the freezing waters. His first child had died. He was bankrupt. He was discredited. He was jobless. He had a wife and a newborn daughter, yet he felt hopeless.

In an epiphany, he realized that his life belonged not to himself but to others. He chose that moment to embark upon an experiment to discover what a little, penniless, unknown individual might be able to do on behalf of humanity. He thought, *If my life belongs not to myself but to others, then what can I do for others? What will become of a life of service?* Over the next fifty-four years, he proved time and again that his most controversial ideas were practical and workable.

DO BATTLE WITH THE CHALLENGES OF
YOUR PRESENT, AND YOU WILL UNLOCK
THE PRIZES OF YOUR FUTURE.

Imagine! A man who is bankrupt, discredited, jobless, and about to commit suicide. And he decides to make his life an experiment! *My life doesn't belong to me; it belongs to others. So I will give it to others.* What happens to a man with nothing who decides to give his life in service?

During the course of this experiment, he was awarded twenty-five U.S. patents, authored twenty-eight books, and received forty-seven honorary doctorates in the arts, sciences, engineering, and humanities. He received dozens of architectural and design awards, including the Gold Medal from the American Institute of Architects and the Gold Medal of the Royal Institute of British Architects. He created work that remains in the permanent collections of museums around the world. He went from a man who was bankrupt, discredited, and about to commit suicide, to a successful speaker who circled the globe fifty-seven times, reaching millions through his lectures, interviews, and work. He decided, *I will live a life of service.*

Creating wealth, even *choosing* wealth, begins with a servant's attitude.

THE LEGACY EXPERIMENT

What if your life was an experiment? What is the legacy you would like to leave? How will you serve generations to come?

> Your choices will determine the answers to this ques-
> tion. Capture your living legacy right now in your journal.

REAL TRAVELER PROFILE: BOB HOPE

Everyone has heroes. One of mine happens to be Bob Hope. Bob
Hope was an extraordinary entertainer, starring in more than
fifty-six movies and more than five hundred Bob Hope Specials.
He entertained American military personnel all over the world for
more than half a century! His commitment to our country, the
tireless schedule he kept, and the freshness he worked to bring to
his comedy are only a few of the things I admired about this man.

Here's a personal correspondence from Bob Hope.

Dear Andy,

You know I've been awfully lucky these last fifty years in show
business, but I had my other tough moments. For instance . . .

Around 1928, I went into Evansville, Indiana, to do an act. I
was having some breakfast, so I looked at the paper to see what
kind of billing I had at the theatre, and it said, *Ben Hope*! So I took
the paper, and I rushed into the theatre. I said to the manager,
"What's the idea of spelling my name that way?"

"What name?"

"Ben Hope! What kind of thing is that?"

"Well, what is your name?"

"Bob Hope."

"Well, who knows?"

I guess at that time nobody knew, and nobody cared, but I got
a pretty good break because at least I was working a few places.

Now about six months before that, I was standing in front of the Woods Theatre Building in Chicago. I had been getting ten dollars a show, but I couldn't even get that. Nobody knew me. My name was Lester Hope, so I decided to change it to Bob Hope 'cause it sounded more chummy, but I still starved. I couldn't book a date.

I wasn't eating very well, and my laundry was piling up. I was just about ready to go home to Cleveland to get a full meal and my laundry cleaned when this friend of mine walked up.

He was a very successful Vaudevillian, Charlie Cooley, and he said, "How you doing?"

"I'm starving."

"Come with me."

And he took me up and introduced me to Charlie Hogan, his booker. He booked small theatres in and around Chicago. He said, "I can give you one day at the West Inglewood Theatre; will twenty-five dollars be all right?"

Well, I gulped, because I'd only been making ten a show at that time. That was the date that got me rolling.

Andy, we all have our slack moments, and they're interesting to look back on. It sort of levels you off a little bit.

I'll see you down in Port Arthur.

Good luck,

Bob Hope

Bob Hope

THREE

THE ACTIVE DECISION

I AM A PERSON OF ACTION.

My future is immediate. I will grasp it in both hands and carry it with running feet. When I am faced with the choice of doing nothing or doing something, I will always choose to act!

The Active Decision for personal success is crucial to you right now. Becoming a person of action is a choice, not a process. You either are a person of action or you are not. It's time to state your case: what are you?

I AM A PERSON OF ACTION.

Beginning today, I will create a new future by creating a new me. No longer will I dwell in a pit of despair, moaning over squandered time and lost opportunity. I can do nothing about the past. My future is immediate. I will grasp it in both hands and carry it with running feet. When I am faced with the choice of doing nothing or doing something, I will always choose to act! I seize this moment. I choose now.

I am a person of action. I am energetic. I move quickly.

Knowing that laziness is a sin, I will create a habit of lively behavior. I will walk with a spring in my step and a smile on my face. The lifeblood rushing through my veins is urging me upward and forward into activity and accomplishment. Wealth and prosperity hide from the sluggard, but rich rewards come to the person who moves quickly.

I am a person of action. I inspire others with my activity. I am a leader.

Leading is doing. To lead, I must move forward. Many people move out of the way for a person on the run; others are caught up in his wake. My activity will create a wave of success for the people who follow. My activity will be consistent. This will instill confidence in my leadership. As a leader, I have the ability to encourage and inspire others to greatness. It is true: an army of sheep led by a lion would defeat an army of lions led by a sheep!

I am a person of action. I can make a decision. I can make it now.

A person who moves neither left nor right is destined for mediocrity. When faced with a decision, many people say they are waiting for God. But I understand, in most cases, God is waiting for me! He has given me a healthy mind to gather and sort information and the courage to come to a conclusion. I am not a quivering dog, indecisive and fearful. My constitution is strong and my pathway clear. Successful people make their decisions quickly and change their minds slowly. Failures make their decisions slowly and change their minds quickly. My decisions come quickly, and they lead to victory.

I am a person of action. I am daring. I am courageous.

Fear no longer has a place in my life. For too long, fear has outweighed my desire to make things better for my family. Never again! I have exposed fear as a vapor, an impostor who never had any power over me in the first place! I do not fear opinion, gossip, or the idle chatter of monkeys, for all are the same to me. I do not fear failure; for in my life, failure is a myth. Failure exists only for the person who quits. I do not quit.

I am courageous. I am a leader. I seize this moment. I choose now.

THE DECISION TO ACT

Without action, none of the other Decisions are useful. People often respond to the notion of action with, "Oh, yeah, I know. I need to take action."

We know! We've all been told, "You have to do something, whether it's right or wrong. It's better to do something than nothing."

Remember that *we* make something happen. Ironically, what's the first thing most people do when they get depressed? What's the first thing people do when they're experiencing hard times? They lie down on the couch, turn on the television, and metaphorically say, "Hit me!" Just like a deer in the headlights.

Always remember that our encouragement, opportunities, knowledge, and information will come from other people—and most of them aren't sitting on the couch when we're depressed! We have to get out and do something.

There are people in your life every day, watching to determine who you are. Be a person of action! Seize moments; choose immediacy. You weren't given the ability to make right decisions all the time, but you were given the ability to make a decision and make it right!

It drives me nuts when I hear people say, "But I can't *always* do my best work." If you can't do your best work, then do your second-best work. But whatever you do, move! Get going!

A person who doesn't move is destined for mediocrity. As I said before, when faced with a decision, I often hear people say, "I'm waiting on God."

I promise you, in most cases, God is waiting on you! Yes, God feeds the birds, but He doesn't throw the worms in their nests. He's given you a healthy mind to gather and sort information, and the courage to come to a conclusion.

> WHEN FACED WITH A DECISION, MANY
> PEOPLE SAY THEY ARE WAITING FOR GOD.
> BUT WE MUST UNDERSTAND THAT, IN
> MOST CASES, GOD IS WAITING FOR US!

THE ACTIVE DECISION

Successful people make their decisions quickly and change their minds slowly. Unsuccessful people make their decisions slowly and change their minds quickly.

Be a person of action. Be daring and courageous! And don't let fear get the best of you.

Fear is nothing but a misuse of the creativity God instilled in you. Fear may have outweighed your desire to make things better for your family. Never let it happen again! Take back your power and expose fear as a vapor—an impostor that never had any power over you in the first place. Never fear opinion, gossip, or the idle chatter of monkeys. Never fear failure—failure is a myth. Failure exists only for those who quit. *You don't quit.*

HISTORY REMEMBERS THE BOLD

The prevailing attitude in our society seems to be "Wait and see." "Don't make a mistake." "Slow down." "Be careful." How significant then could it be to actually *do* something? Remember the old Indian proverb? "Man who stand on top of mountain with mouth open wait long time for roast turkey to fly in."

History chronicles the bold and the timid, but it's the bold we remember. The bold capture our imagination, inspiring us as we move through our own lives. We remember people like Susan B. Anthony, Henry Ford, the Wright brothers, Florence Nightingale, and modern giants like Lee Iacocca, Bill Gates, Oprah Winfrey, Warren Buffett, and Jack Welch. These bold people, with the courage of their convictions, seize the moment. They demonstrate that difficulties disappear and obstacles vanish in the face of unwavering courage. The bold capture our hearts and souls because they have followed their hearts to become who they are, providing a shining path for us to follow.

During the Olympics, we are enamored with the courage of

53

the bold. And it's not necessarily the ones who win the events who inspire us but the ones who compete with their hearts at an uncommon level. We recognize the hero within ourselves when the athlete gives everything he has, including his last breath and finishes, limping off the field of battle.

Do you remember what Ulysses S. Grant, the eighteenth president of the United States, looked like? You probably have seen one or more portraits of him and do remember his looks. Did you know that he never held any political office other than president of the United States? And yet we remember him very clearly.

Do you remember what Rutherford B. Hayes looked like? What about James Garfield, Chester Arthur, or Grover Cleveland? Do you remember Benjamin Harrison or William McKinley? Probably not. Yet, amazingly, each of these men served as president of the United States *after* Ulysses S. Grant. Grant has been dead more than a hundred years, but you recall what he looked like and may even have a good idea of his personality.

MANY PEOPLE MOVE OUT OF THE WAY
FOR A PERSON ON THE RUN; OTHERS
ARE CAUGHT UP IN HIS WAKE.

Grant was a general in the Union army during the Civil War. But did you know he wasn't the first one? Or the second or the third or the fourth or even the fifth? He was the *tenth* general Lincoln appointed during the Civil War. Why do you remember him? Because he was a person of action.

Winfield Scott was Lincoln's first general. Next came McDowell, followed by Fremont, then the disastrous George McClellan. In McClellan, Lincoln had a commander of the entire Union army who refused to engage the enemy! After McClellan, Lincoln appointed Henry Halleck, a graduate of West Point and a published author on military tactics. Lincoln read the book—a fine book with good theory—right before he appointed Halleck. Lincoln found out books don't fight wars. Halleck evaded all personal responsibility, lost what little composure he brought to the task, and eventually became nothing more than a clerk.

After Lincoln appointed Rosecrans, McClernand was next in line. According to Lincoln, all McClernand did was complain about the other generals, almost weekly, in a long, rambling communication critical of something Sherman or the other generals had done.

Burnside was next, then Banks. The day Lincoln announced his intentions to promote General Ulysses S. Grant, he was vilified in the press. Even after Grant was appointed, the press was pushing for Grant's dismissal, but Lincoln couldn't spare him because Grant was thoughtful, he moved forward, and he was bold in his tactics. He was a person of action. One of the big criticisms of Grant at the time was that he drank too much. Lincoln said privately, "Well, if I can find out what he's drinking, I'll send a few cases to the other generals."

OVERCOMING FEAR

Fear debilitates action. Where has fear hindered your progress? Has fear kept you from pursuing a job promotion, diving into a new career, going after a big account, reinventing your business, or innovating? Fear of failure, humiliation, or making mistakes hinders our creative impulses and our ability to create extraordinary changes in the world.

Step 1: To overcome fear, we must first identify it.

Identify five places in your life and business where fear has hindered your progress.

When the tiger is charging you, two choices arise: stand motionless in fear to be mauled, or attack the tiger and see what happens. In standing motionless your fate is certain. In attacking the tiger a myriad of possibilities exist, including the tiger becoming afraid (or simply thinking you're insane) and running away. The point is, we must push through our fears to grow and become more.

Step 2: What if fear was no longer a factor? State an affirmative decision for each of the fears you listed in Step 1. What actions are you committed to taking (on a consistent basis) to make your fears irrelevant? Create a list of action steps for moving beyond each fear.

THE WAY OF THE HERO

Calvin Coolidge stated, "We can't do everything at once, but, by God, we can do something at once!" Changing the world begins with a single act.

Do you remember the story of a twelve-year-old from Tacoma, Washington, named J. J. Rousch? J. J. was a hero. He had stopped a fire in his aunt and uncle's house in Midland, just outside of Tacoma. The national news called him a hero, and J. J.'s parents and his aunt and uncle certainly agreed. But J. J. didn't really think he was much of a hero because he didn't really think about what he was doing.

When smoke poured from his aunt and uncle's house, he reacted. Following his mother's orders, J. J. grabbed a sixty-five-pound fire extinguisher from his grandma's house nearby, and this twelve-year-old rushed over to the house on fire, grabbed a ten-pound object outside the back door, and hurled it through the kitchen window. As his mother used the extinguisher on the fire, the boy grabbed a garden hose, kicked in the front door, and battled the flames with water. When the firefighters arrived, the blaze was out.

AN ARMY OF SHEEP LED BY A LION WOULD DEFEAT AN ARMY OF LIONS LED BY A SHEEP!

Curiously, there were people who witnessed this event who simply watched because they didn't really know what to do. As J. J. said later, "All I thought was, 'Oh, wow, a fire.'"

Then he kicked the door in and battled the flames while everybody else was wondering what to do. "I'm not really a hero. I didn't really think of myself as a hero. I didn't really think at all," J. J. said.

But that is precisely why this twelve-year-old boy is a hero— because he didn't stop to think; he just acted.

Remember the story of the Kentucky Boy Scout from Bowling Green? Matt Knight was practicing with his cross-country team at a park when he stopped to tie his shoe. From across the park, he heard the screams of Susan Beth Meeks, an eighth-grader who had fallen into a pipe at the end of the drainage ditch. Her foot was lodged under a rock, forcing her head underwater while she struggled to escape. Matt found her, slid into the pipe, ducked his head under the water, and pushed her out. Matt said later that he was nervous as he jumped into the pipe with the struggling girl, "but I had to do something, so I did."

For Matt's act, he received the Honor Medal with Crossed Palms from the Boy Scouts of America. Since the medal's creation in the 1930s, only 166 people have received it. He then went to the White House and met the president of the United States, who congratulated him on his heroism. Certainly, Susan calls him her hero, but to Matt, he was just acting rather than wondering what to do.

Action is a choice. Interestingly, Matt, a sophomore in high school, made the choice to act long before the crisis. In subsequent interviews, he said, "I had thought about what would happen if I was ever faced with an emergency. I determined right away I would do whatever came to mind to solve the problem."

So are you ready for your moment? Have you decided what you will do when your moment arrives? We've heard over and over again that success happens when preparation meets opportunity.

THE DEATHBED EXERCISE

Write a glowing, incredible eulogy you would like to have read aloud at your funeral. Here are some key questions to help:

- What was your life's work about?
- Who was affected as a result of your actions?
- Who was made a better person because of you?
- What were the three biggest events that happened because of you?
- For what will you be remembered?
- How was the world different because of you?

Write your eulogy in your journal; then type and print it. Carry it with you wherever you go.

1. Share your eulogy with the three most important people in your life. Ask them for their feedback

and suggestions on what needs to happen for you to become the person in the eulogy. Practically speaking, to make your eulogy a reality, where do you begin?

2. Put your eulogy into a Microsoft PowerPoint presentation to help you visualize what you want to do. Your mind often thinks in pictures, and having a visual presentation of your eulogy will help you keep it in mind.

This exercise will help you clarify what you want your life's accomplishments to be and help you build momentum to achieve them.

BECOMING A PERSON OF ACTION

You are a person of action. Too many people, when faced with a choice, lie down on the couch and watch TV. We live in a deer-in-the-headlights world, where people facing tough situations basically say, "Roll over me."

The Active Decision affirms: "I am a person of action. I seize this moment. I choose now!" Beginning today, you are going to create a new future by creating a new you. There's no reason to dwell in the pit of despair or moan over squandered time or lost opportunities. You can't do anything about the past. Your future lies before you. Grasp it with both hands and run with it! When you're faced with the choice to do nothing or do something, you will always choose to act. Seize this moment. Choose now!

Leading is doing. To lead, you have to move forward, to be ahead of other people. By being a person of action, you'll inspire others and become a natural leader. People move out of the way for a person on the run, and other people are caught up in the runner's wake. Your activity creates a wave of success for people who follow. Your activity, actions, and movements must be consistent, for consistent action instills confidence in your leadership. People follow a person on the move. Leaders encourage and inspire others to greatness. They watch what you do. *An army of sheep led by a lion will defeat an army of lions led by a sheep every time.*

EMBRACING THE POWER OF ACTION

In the Realizing Your Future Identity exercise, page 20 in the Responsible Decision, you identified the person you need to become in order to realize your Ultimate Vision. Now, you need to identify the steps to take today, tomorrow, and in the weeks, months, and years to come to help move you toward that self-actualized person.

Quickly scan what you wrote for both the Crafting Your Ultimate Vision (page 18) and Realizing Your Future Identity exercises. Next, capture ten things you can do in the next twenty-four hours to move you in that direction. A simple action such as picking up the phone and reconnecting with an old friend can help you build tremendous momentum toward your desired destination.

Who can you call? What can you research? What book do you need to read? What action can you take to help move you toward your Ultimate Vision? List ten actions you are committed to taking in the next twenty-four to forty-eight hours.

CHAMBERLAIN'S CHARGE

Andrew Jackson, our seventh president, said, "Take time to be deliberate, but when the time for action arrives, stop thinking and go in!"

Did you know that one guy 150 years ago made a move that changed how our nation operates within this world? This one man's story was told in *The Traveler's Gift*, but it bears retelling here.

On the hot, humid day of July 2, 1863, Joshua Lawrence Chamberlain, a thirty-four-year-old schoolteacher from Maine and former professor of rhetoric from Bowdoin College, was in the fight of his life. He stood at the far left edge of a group of eighty thousand men strung out in a line across fields and hills, stretching all the way to a little town called Gettysburg, Pennsylvania.

Earlier in the day, Colonel Vincent placed Chamberlain and the men of the Twentieth Maine at the end of the line, saying, "Whatever you do, you can't let them through here." Chamberlain couldn't withdraw, and he knew it. If the Confederate army over-ran them, the rebels would barricade the high ground, and the Union's Army of the Potomac would forfeit. In essence, eighty thousand men would be caught from behind on a downhill charge with no protection. To win, the rebels would have to come through Chamberlain. Chamberlain knew he could not retreat.

SUCCESSFUL PEOPLE MAKE THEIR DECISIONS
QUICKLY AND CHANGE THEIR MINDS SLOWLY.
UNSUCCESSFUL PEOPLE MAKE THEIR DECISIONS
SLOWLY AND CHANGE THEIR MINDS QUICKLY.

At 2:30 p.m., the first charge came from the Fifteenth and Forty-Seventh Alabama, running uphill as fast as they could and firing at Chamberlain's men, stationed on a rock wall they had thrown up earlier that day. Chamberlain's men pushed them back and did again on a second and third charge. On the fourth charge, Chamberlain took a bullet to his belt buckle. He fell over, got back up, and kept fighting. Again they pushed the Confederate troops down the hill.

At that point in our nation's history, battles were fought with artillery and ammunition, and you could see your enemy's faces as they surged up the hill. Chamberlain and his men had stacked up a rock wall of pie-plate-sized rocks 110 yards long. On that fourth charge, the rebels almost breached the wall.

Chamberlain, while waiting for the next charge, thought, *I'm a professor of rhetoric. I'm fairly certain I don't have anything anyone would care to learn at this point.*

He recalled, "Later, I felt sorry for my men. Their leader had no real knowledge of warfare or tactics. I was only a stubborn man, and that was my greatest advantage in this fight. I had, deep within me, the inability to do nothing."

Chamberlain continued, "I knew I may die, but I knew that I would not die with a bullet in my back. I would not die in retreat. I am, at least, like the apostle Paul, who wrote, 'This one thing I do, I press toward the mark.'" The attack came again. On the fifth charge, the men of the Fifteenth and Forty-Seventh Alabama broke the wall open. They were fighting on both sides of the wall. Chamberlain's men couldn't reload. They were almost out of ammunition anyway, so they were swinging guns at each other and hitting with their fists. Somehow Chamberlain's men pushed the enemy back again.

After pushing the enemy down the hill five times, Chamberlain's brother, Tom, came running up with Sergeant Tozier, an old, hard-nosed soldier. Tozier had a thick wad of torn shirt stuck into a hole in his shoulder where he had been wounded.

"No help from the Eighty-Third," he said. "They're shot to ribbons, and all they can do is extend the line a bit. We're getting murdered on our flank."

"Can we extend?" Chamberlain asked.

His brother, Tom, said, "There's nothing to extend! More than half our men are down."

Chamberlain's company had started in Bangor, Maine, six months earlier, with a thousand men. They'd started that morning with three hundred. Now they were down to eighty.

"How are we for ammunition?" he said.

"We've been shooting a lot," was his answer.

Chamberlain said, "I know we've been shooting a lot. I want to know how we're holding out. What kind of ammunition have we got?"

As his brother went to check, the twelve-year-old lookout who had climbed a tree yelled, "They're forming up again, Colonel."

Chamberlain looked up to see the boy pointing down the hill. "They're forming up right now. And they've been reinforced. Sir, there's a lot more of them this time."

"Sir!" Sergeant Thomas stumbled into their midst, out of breath. "Colonel Chamberlain, sir. Sir! Colonel Vincent is dead."

"Are you sure, soldier?"

"Yes, sir," he said. "He was shot right at the first of the fight. They were firmed up by Weeds Brigade up front, but now Weeds is dead. They moved Hazlett's Battery up top. Hazlett's dead."

His brother came running back. "Joshua," he said, "we're out! One, two rounds per man at the most. Some of the men don't have anything at all."

Chamberlain turned to a thin man standing at his right. It was First Sergeant Ellis Spear. "Spear," he said, "tell the boys to take the ammunition from the wounded and the dead."

Chamberlain's men started wondering where they were going

and what was going to happen. Spear replied, "Maybe we should think about pulling out, sir."

Chamberlain retorted grimly, "We will not be pulling out, Sergeant. Carry out my orders, please."

"Colonel!" Sergeant Tozier spoke up. "Sir, we won't hold them again. You know we won't."

"Joshua!" It was his brother. "Here they come. Here they come!"

Chamberlain stepped on top of the wall in full view, crossing his arms and staring down at the advancing army. The Fifteenth and Forty-Seventh Alabama with their pale, yellow-gray uniforms, now reinforced by a Texas regiment, moved up the hill, and that high-pitched shriek—the rebel yell—coursed up toward Chamberlain and his men. Sergeant Spear had returned and was standing at Chamberlain's feet. Sergeant Tozier, Chamberlain's brother, and another lieutenant were huddled below. His brother said, "Joshua! Give an order!"

Chamberlain just stood there, deep in thought, quickly sorting the situation. *We can't retreat,* he thought. *We can't stay here. When I'm faced with the choice of doing nothing or doing something, I will always choose to act.* He turned his back on the advancing rebels, looked down at his men, and said, "Fix bayonets!"

Can you imagine being given that command? At first, no one moved. They just stared at him with their mouths open. "We'll have the advantage of moving downhill," Chamberlain said. "Fix the bayonets now and execute a great right wheel of the entire regiment! Swing left first."

The lieutenant spoke up first, confused. "Sir," he asked, "what is a great right wheel?" But the colonel had already jumped from the rocks and was moving to the next group of men.

Sergeant Tozier answered his question. "He means to charge, son. A great right wheel is an all-out charge."

His men watched in awe as Chamberlain drew his sword.

He leaped up onto the wall again and screamed, "Bayonets! Bayonets!"

"I HAD, DEEP WITHIN ME, THE INABILITY TO DO
NOTHING. . . . I KNEW I MAY DIE, BUT I KNEW
I WOULD NOT DIE WITH A BULLET IN MY BACK.
I WOULD NOT DIE IN RETREAT. I AM, AT LEAST,
LIKE THE APOSTLE PAUL, WHO WROTE, 'THIS
ONE THING I DO, I PRESS TOWARD THE MARK.'"

And, turning, the colonel pointed his sword directly down-hill. He wheeled and faced these overwhelming odds, slashed his blade through the air, and with a power born of courage and fear, the schoolteacher from Maine roared, "Charge! Charge! Charge! Charge! Charge!" to his men.

The eighty remaining fighting men of the Twentieth Maine tumbled over the wall after Chamberlain into history. An incredible example of a leader who refused to fail, Chamberlain knew that we move forward or we die. As they rolled over that wall and ran downhill, they lifted their voices to match the voice of their leader. "Charge!" they shouted. "Charge! Charge!"

When the Confederate troops saw Chamberlain, the leader of the opposition, mount that wall, they immediately stopped, unsure of what was happening. And when Chamberlain pointed his sword toward them and commanded his men to charge, they turned and ran. Many of them threw down their loaded weapons. The rebels were certain that these were not the same soldiers they'd been facing. *Surely these men had massive reinforcements*, they must have thought. *A beaten regiment wouldn't charge!* In less than ten minutes, Chamberlain had his sword on the collarbone of a captain in the Confederate army. "You, sir, are my prisoner," he said.

The man turned a loaded pistol around and handed it to Chamberlain and said, "Yes sir. I am."

Ten minutes later, that ragged group of men under Chamberlain's command, without any ammunition, captured more than four hundred soldiers of the enemy.

Historians have determined that, had Chamberlain not charged that day, the South would have won at Gettysburg. If the South had won at Gettysburg, historians say, the South would have won the war. Now, I always thought that if the South had won, we would be the North and South, but historians say that had the South won, we would now have a continent that looks more like Europe, fragmented into nine to thirteen countries. Which means that, had Chamberlain not charged, when Hitler swept across Europe in the 1940s, the United States of America wouldn't have existed to stand in the breach. When Hirohito systematically invaded the islands of the South Pacific, there would not have existed a country big enough, powerful enough, strong, populous, and wealthy enough to fight and win two wars on two fronts at the same time. The United States of America exists today because of one man who made a decision to charge. One man decided that he was a person of action.

EARLY TO BED, EARLY TO RISE . . .

I encourage you to become an early riser. Thomas Jefferson woke up early every day. He said, "Whether I retire to bed early or late, I rise with the sun."

One of our country's founding fathers, Thomas Jefferson had an appetite for action. He said, "Do you want to know who you are? Don't ask. Act. Action will delineate and define you." He also said, "Determine never to be idle. It is wonderful how much may be done if we are always doing." Another one of Jefferson's great quotes: "I'm a great believer in luck; and I find the harder I work, the more I have of it."

Thomas Jefferson knew that action made the man. He managed more than ten thousand acres as a farmer. He became a surveyor and a successful land speculator. He owned a profitable nail factory. He was an extraordinary horseman who was still riding two months before his death at eighty-three. He was an accomplished architect who designed his own home and the homes of many of his friends.

He founded the University of Virginia, designed the campus, hired the professors, and wrote the curriculum. He was a respected and published naturalist, horticulturist, and meteorologist. He was a chess player, an accomplished singer, and a violin player—he is believed to have owned a Stradivarius. He was the president of the American Philosophical Society for twenty years, as well as a regent and alumnus of William and Mary College.

He was a diligent correspondent, and more than twenty-eight thousand of his letters survived. He was fluent in Latin, Greek, French, and Italian. He studied Anglo-Saxon, German, and American Indian dialects. He was a voracious reader and book collector, with a library of twenty-seven hundred volumes by age forty. He was the creator of the Library of Congress, the U.S. Patent Office, and the U.S. monetary system.

Jefferson was a practicing lawyer and two-term governor of the Commonwealth of Virginia. He was the U.S. minister to France for five years and the first U.S. secretary of state. He was both vice president and president of the United States, and he authored what many consider the most important document ever written: the Declaration of Independence.

There was a fifty-year period in Jefferson's life during which the sun never caught him in bed. He rose as soon as he could read the hands on the clock next to his bed. George Washington Carver also rose early. He said he did so he could talk to God and find out what His instructions were for the day. Benjamin Franklin crafted the maxim, "Early to bed and early to rise makes a man healthy, wealthy, and wise." This is more than just a quote; it's really true!

Challenge yourself to wake up early until it's a habit. Waking up before the rest of the world is a doorway to new and creative ideas. It's a biblical principle too. Romans 13:11–12 says, "Knowing the time, that now it is high time to awake out of sleep. . . . The night is far spent, the day is at hand: let us therefore cast off the works of darkness, and let us put on the armour of light" (KJV).

30-DAY EARLY-TO-RISE CHALLENGE

I present you with the "30-Day Early-to-Rise Challenge"—an activity that will change your life if you follow through with it. For thirty days, get up at least an hour before the rest of the house. (Go to bed earlier if you need to, but you'll probably find you don't need to.)

Your objective when you wake up in the morning is to come up with several new ideas that inspire and motivate you. Keep a pen and a journal nearby and jot down the first twenty ideas that come to mind. Write quickly. Chalkboard. Brainstorm. Circle the idea that is most important to you. To set that idea in motion, quickly brainstorm five specific actions you can take within twenty-four hours and do them.

Over thirty days you'll have come up with thirty new

---

ideas. Any one of these can take your life in an incredible new direction.

(Don't panic! I'm not saying this is something that you have to do for the rest of your life. You can occasionally sleep in after the thirty days.)

THE BUTTERFLY'S EFFECT ON CHANGE

The beautiful thing about taking action is that each action you take changes things. Every time you do something, it matters, and I can prove it. When you grasp this concept, you will begin to truly appreciate your value as well as the value of others in the world. Every single thing we do matters—forever. And yet, most of us don't see this. Instead, it seems that some people are more important than others, and some of us are not needed at all. And some people believe they can do things all by themselves.

> FEAR NO LONGER HAS A PLACE IN MY
> LIFE. . . . I HAVE EXPOSED FEAR AS A VAPOR,
> AN IMPOSTOR WHO NEVER HAD ANY POWER
> OVER ME IN THE FIRST PLACE! . . . I DO NOT
> FEAR FAILURE, FOR IN MY LIFE, FAILURE
> IS A MYTH. FAILURE EXISTS ONLY FOR THE
> PERSON WHO QUITS. I DO NOT QUIT.

I love convincing the CEO of a major corporation that the man or woman answering the phones isn't just the receptionist but the "director of first impressions" for the entire company. The CEO could vacation for three or four weeks, and we may not even know he or she is gone, but if the director of first impressions takes the afternoon off, the business might shut down! We all are important.

Have you heard of the butterfly effect? The butterfly effect was the subject of a doctoral thesis written in 1963, by Edward Lorenz. According to him, the butterfly effect posited that the butterfly could flap its wings and set molecules of air in motion that could eventually create a hurricane on the other side of the world. The butterfly effect was laughed out of the New York Academy of Science because everyone saw it as ridiculous.

But it *was* interesting. The theory hung around as urban legend until the midnineties, when physics professors proved the butterfly effect was accurate and viable. In fact, the butterfly effect worked with every form of moving matter, including people. Like the law of gravity, the butterfly effect was given the status of a law because it worked every time. It is now known as the law of sensitive dependence upon initial conditions.

Joshua Chamberlain is an excellent example of the butterfly effect. One man made one move 150 years ago, and the effects of his actions are still rippling through all of our lives today.

THE PROTECTIVE FIELD OF PURPOSE

It occurs to me that as you read this, you might be going through the worst time in your life. If that's the case, know that it's normal. *We all are either in a crisis, coming out of a crisis, or headed for a crisis.* It's just part of being on this planet. Things may feel horrible right now, but you are still here. And if you're *here*, you haven't finished what you were put here to do.

The greatest part of your life—your purpose—has yet to be lived. There is more fun to have! There's more success to experience. There's more laughter to enjoy. There are more children to teach and more friends to influence and help. And if what you were put here to do hasn't been completed, you can't be harmed. There is a protection around you just like there was around Chamberlain. When the bullet found its mark on Chamberlain, it hit his belt buckle. He got proof (just like you'll see proof) that until you accomplish what you were put here to do, you will not and cannot be harmed.

Chamberlain would later serve four terms as governor of Maine. During the third term, he received further confirmation of the divine protection that surrounded him. A letter arrived at the state house addressed to Governor Joshua Chamberlain from a member of the Fifteenth Alabama:

Dear Sir,

I want to tell you of a little passage in the battle of Round Top, Gettysburg, concerning you and me which I am now glad of. Twice in that fight I had your life in my hands. I got a safe place between two rocks and drew bead fair and square on you. You were standing in the open, behind the center of your line, fully exposed. I knew your rank by your uniform and accents, and I thought it a mighty good thing to put you out of the way. I rested my gun on the rock and took steady aim. I started to pull the trigger, but some strange notion stopped me. Then I got ashamed of my weakness and went through the same motions again. I had you perfectly certain. But that same strange something shut right down on me. I couldn't pull the trigger and gave it up. That is, your life. I am glad of it now and hope you are.

Yours truly,
A Member of the 15th Alabama

There will be protection around you as you act and move and become what you were meant to be. You may never see it, but I can promise you this: there is no need to live the rest of your life—any part of your life—in fear.

CAPITALIZING ON YOUR STRENGTHS

We each excel in certain areas. Some of us are fast runners. Some of us are sharp thinkers. Others might be better at managing finances. Some are confident communicators. Some are caring, loving, and uplifting. Some are loyal. You get the idea.

We don't want to only identify areas we need to improve; we want to capitalize on our God-given strengths! If we capitalize on our current strengths, we can create momentum and take on the challenges that await us.

Clarify what you're great at—what you do best and enjoy most. What's your "hot zone"? What are your current areas of mastery? List your strengths in your journal.

ADAMS'S CHOICE

John Adams was more than just our second president—the accomplishments of his life massively shaped our world. He was a servant who proclaimed, "If we do not lay ourselves out in the service of mankind, whom should we serve?"

John Adams had a purpose far beyond his own life. He believed that it wasn't words or reactions but *actions* that make the person. There was a new law going around the colonies that could have easily ruined Adams: the colonists refused to purchase stamped paper while the British governor refused to acknowledge legal documents without the stamps. Although this basically cut off Adams's income as an attorney, he stood with the colonists even when some fellow "patriots" stood only when it didn't affect their pocketbooks. To Adams, his stand was critical because it was aligned with the words of Thomas Jefferson in one of the most potent documents ever created—the Declaration of Independence: "And for the support of this declaration with a firm reliance on the protection of divine providence, we mutually pledge to each other our lives, our fortunes, and our sacred honor."

What can you learn from the example of one of our greatest presidents? Greatness comes at a cost. What will you have to give up to get what you want? Will it be time? Will it be petty habits or limiting beliefs? Will you have to give up your fears? Remember: thoughts don't change anything until they are acted upon. Action changes everything.

Adams saw himself as more than just a Harvard-educated man, a great lawyer, a husband to Abigail, or a president to a nation. Adams saw himself as a shaper of the future. He knew his actions would affect many; therefore he acted and spoke in a manner consistent with this understanding. What if you believe today that your actions will affect millions of people? How will you act and speak? How must you act and speak now to make not only your dreams but the dreams of millions come true? John Adams knew his role. He said, "I must study politics and war, that my sons may have liberty to study mathematics and philosophy." He was giving something for the future. He didn't really want to study politics and war, but in his mind he had to so his children would have the freedom to study what they wanted.

YOUR ROLES IN ACTION

John Adams knew his role: "I must study politics and war, that my sons may have liberty to study mathematics and philosophy."

> How do you see yourself? Write down three roles that you feel identify who you are and what your life is about (visionary businessman, extraordinary father/mother, and so on).
>
> What specific actions can you take that are linked to each of these roles?

REAL TRAVELER PROFILE: STAN LEE

If you have ever read a comic book or seen a comic hero–based action movie, you've most likely experienced the vivid imagination of Stan Lee. The former chairman of Marvel Comics and Marvel Films and now cofounder of POW! Entertainment, Stan Lee is perhaps the most influential personality in the comic book industry. Legendary characters like Spider-Man, the Incredible Hulk, the Fantastic Four, and the X-Men were all conceived in Lee's brilliant mind.

It's easy to assume that such an extraordinary innovator would have little trouble starting his career. "Hey, this guy created Spider-Man. I'm sure he didn't have any trouble getting work." The path of the *Traveler*, however, is always checkered with failure and adversity.

Here's a personal correspondence from Stan Lee.

Hi, Andy,

I've rarely followed anyone else's advice in my lifetime, so I don't know why you would want to follow mine, but for what it's worth, here's a thought you might want to play with . . .

You neither learn nor grow by your successes, only by your failures. Failure is the grease that keeps the world's engines running. It's the adrenaline that sparks the human condition, that keeps us grasping and groping and growing. But, you have to know how to deal with failure—and, most importantly, how to free yourself of its yoke. Case in point . . .

For the first twenty years of my career in comic books, I tried in vain to sell a comic strip to the major newspaper syndicates. I wanted to be right up there with the guys who created Dick Tracy, Terry and the Pirates, and Flash Gordon. But, for that entire twenty-year period, I received rejection after rejection. Talk about failure—I was its poster boy! Did I quit? Did I figure I was wasting my time? Did I give up? Damn right I did! [NOTE: Actually, Stan is just being poetic. He didn't give up; he just changed his approach to getting what he wanted!]

I then devoted all my energies to making my comic books as good as they could be. [Stan Lee chose the Active Decision, which led to a turning point.] And what happened? After I stopped wasting time collecting rejection strips from newspaper syndicates and started concentrating on what I did best, Spider-Man, the Incredible Hulk and all our other Marvel heroes made it big. They became world famous.

And then it happened! The syndicates came after me! No more writing countless letters or endlessly knocking on doors— now I could pick and choose which syndicate I deigned to allow to represent me!

That taught me an unforgettable lesson. I'm just sorry it took me twenty years to learn it. Persistence is a great virtue. Whatever it is you're trying to accomplish, you should never give up while there's a shred of hope left. But . . .

You must also be perceptive enough to know when something just isn't going to work. There has to be a time when you let it go and look for other opportunities—the world is filled with them. Not everybody makes it in every endeavor. Not everybody gets to grab the gold ring in a chosen field. Just as it's important not to

give up so long as you have a fighting chance, it's equally important to know when to stop wasting time trying for an impossible
goal. It's sometimes better to switch gears, change your direction, and find another challenge, one which has a better chance
of success.

The trick is not to get hooked on failure. You don't need that
monkey on your back. If something doesn't work, jump off the
track, take another train. There's a big, wide world out there;
you've got countless options—don't neglect a single one! Just like
me. I suddenly realize that this letter may not be making it, so I'm
smart enough to quit—right now!

All the best,

Stan

Stan Lee

FOUR

THE CERTAIN DECISION

I HAVE A DECIDED HEART.

Truth is truth. If a thousand people believe something foolish, it is still foolish! Truth is never dependent upon consensus of opinion. I have found that it is better to be alone and acting upon the truth in my heart than to follow a gaggle of silly geese doomed to mediocrity.

The Certain Decision for personal success is what fuels your actions from the Active Decision. The clarity of vision you maintain in your mind is directly proportional to the effectiveness of your actions. A decided heart is unwavering in the face of continual challenges and setbacks, and that ensures victory and a lifetime of greater fulfillment.

I HAVE A DECIDED HEART.

A wise man once said, "A journey of a thousand miles begins with a single step." Knowing this to be true, I am taking my first step today. For too long my feet have been tentative, shuffling left and right, more backward than forward as my heart gauged the direction of the wind. Criticism, condemnation, and complaint are creatures of the wind. They come and go on the wasted breath of lesser beings and have no power over me. The power to control direction belongs to me. Today I will begin to exercise that power.

My course has been charted. My destiny is assured.

I have a decided heart. I am passionate about my vision for the future.

I will awaken every morning with an excitement about the new day and its opportunity for growth and change. My thoughts and actions will work in a forward motion, never sliding into the dark forest of doubt or the muddy quicksand of self-pity. I will freely give my vision for the future to others, and as they see the belief in my eyes, they will follow me.

I will lay my head on my pillow at night happily exhausted, knowing that I have done everything within my power to move the mountains in my path. As I sleep, the same dream that dominates my waking hours will be with me in the dark. Yes, I have a dream. It is a great dream, and I will never apologize for it. Neither will I ever let it go, for if I did, my life would be finished. My hopes, my passions, my vision for the future are my very existence. A person without a dream never had a dream come true.

I have a decided heart. I will not wait.

I know that the purpose of analysis is to come to a conclusion. I have tested the angles. I have measured the probabilities. And now I have made a decision with my heart. I am not timid. I will move now and not look back. What I put off until tomorrow, I will put off until the next day as well. I do not procrastinate. All my problems become smaller when I confront them. If I touch a thistle with caution, it will prick me, but if I grasp it boldly, its spines crumble into dust.

I will not wait. I am passionate about my vision for the future. My course has been charted. My destiny is assured.

I have a decided heart.

THE PURPOSE OF ANALYSIS

The fourth Decision states: *I have a decided heart.* More people fail at what they attempt because of an undecided heart than for any other reason. We all know people who make decisions with an undecided heart. They'll tell you about a decision they're trying to make, lament over the various options, ask for your opinion, and then talk to someone else about their decision, asking for more opinions! "What do you think? Left? Right? Up? Down? Orange? Green?" They even get opinions about the first opinion they got. "What do you think about what this guy said?"

Then they take the decision back to their friends to discuss whether they should change their decision or stick with it. Life becomes an ongoing state of analysis.

But get this: *the purpose of analysis is to come to a conclusion!* It's not to continue to analyze. Get to it! To repeat what I've said before, successful people make their decisions quickly and change their minds slowly. Unsuccessful people make their decisions slowly and change their minds quickly. Many people spend so much time analyzing the decisions they have already made that they don't have any energy left to actually do what they decided!

The prospect of making a "right decision" scares people. I don't believe we can make right decisions all the time unless we were born with the ability to tell the future (which I won't believe until I see a newspaper headline, "Psychic Wins Lottery"). Unless you can tell the future, you couldn't possibly gather enough information to make right decisions all the time. We are, however, as we stated earlier, made with the ability to *make a decision and then go about the business of making it right.*

A DECIDED HEART

The great evangelist Billy Graham brilliantly noted, "I'm always amazed at how many people in trouble confuse God's will for their life with plain old bad decision making." The wisdom in that statement is profound, revealing how many people misunderstand the Certain Decision.

I have a decided heart. My destiny is assured.

So what is a decided heart? A decided heart has to do with how we make decisions and our conduct after that decision is made; it has nothing to do with action or persistence.

We all know people who get locked into endless analysis, never moving past the decision-making avalanche. The endless opinion-gathering process and uncertainty gathers momentum, like a snowball rolling downhill, getting bigger and bigger as the analysis gets more complex. When they finally make a decision, the analysis continues.

Although there are questions that cannot be answered, they can be decided. Remember, most of the time you won't have all the facts you need to give you a complete picture. You will, however, have all the facts you need to make a decision.

Do you remember the leadership discussion we had in the introduction?

"Where do you want to go eat?"

"I don't know. Where do you want to go eat?"

"Truly . . . wherever you want to go . . ."

Note that the people who make a decision and then make it right are the people we admire in our society. They have decided hearts, and their destiny is assured.

Do you know people who are absolutely sure that God has led them down a certain path until it gets tough, and then they're just as sure that God has led them in the opposite direction? If you know people who are determined to live their lives in that netherworld of wishy-washy decision making, tell them God said to leave Him out of it!

God doesn't change His mind. Did you know that even the Bible says wishy-washy people are dangerous? "A double minded man is unstable in all his ways" (James 1:8 KJV). An indecisive person allows instability into every part of his life. It touches everything—our families, our businesses, our hopes, and our dreams. And if we don't decide what's important in our lives, we're going to end up doing things that are important to other people.

When you exhibit a decided heart and commit yourself to the fulfillment of the destiny you have chosen, your life will never be the same. People will follow you everywhere, seeking your wisdom and advice—all because you have a decided heart. Challenges that you previously thought were mountains in your life melt at your feet when you have a decided heart.

IDENTIFYING YOUR DRIVERS

At this point in our exploration of the Seven Decisions, you've identified numerous areas for growth and even committed to some actions. Now, based on what you've learned about yourself thus far, choose three specific decisions you have made in the course of working through this book.

For each decision, write all the reasons why it is important—why it is a MUST. What will following through on this decision give you? How will your life change? The drivers behind your decisions are what will give you the energy to see them through. The more powerful the driver, the more committed you'll become.

FINDING YOUR VISION

One of the best ways to keep your heart decided is to make sure the destiny you're working toward is worth the hassle. Life can be a struggle. Success as a parent, a friend, a businessperson, or a community contributor, or success at any level and in any arena, can be, and often is, a struggle. It's going to be a struggle to maintain a decided heart; otherwise what you're struggling for isn't worth the struggle in the first place!

Think big! If what you're working toward isn't big enough, you're going to be ambushed by bigger things every day of your life. Remember: If you're hunting rabbits in tiger country, you gotta keep your eyes peeled for the tigers. But if you're hunting tigers, you can just ignore the rabbits!

A MINI—GOAL-SETTING WORKSHOP

You never lack time or money—only an idea. Linus Pauling, the Nobel laureate in chemistry, said, "The best way to get a good idea is to get a lot of ideas."

Now it's time to figure out some of the major goals you want to achieve. In your journal brainstorm a master list of goals you have for this lifetime—big and small. Do you want to write a book? Do you want to run your division? Start a company? Start a family? Travel to Australia? Read more poetry? Take a wine-tasting class? Learn a foreign language? Take a martial arts class? Master calligraphy?

Upon what new adventure do you wish to embark? What new skill must you master?

Your goals should help you move toward the Ultimate Vision of the life you want to create. Capture your goals for your professional and personal life.

YOUR HEART, YOUR LIFE

When I sat down to outline *The Traveler's Gift*, I listed people throughout history who best personified each of the Seven Decisions. When I got to the fourth Decision, "I have a decided heart; my destiny is assured," Christopher Columbus practically leaped out at me. Columbus, with all his failings, epitomized a person with a decided heart. One of the characteristics of a person with a decided heart is that he owns his Decision. "If you're with me, fine; if you're not with me, fine. I am going. I have a decided heart. You can come along for the ride or not. And if you're against me, I do not care what you think or say."

Columbus didn't care what anybody thought or said, and frankly, outside your personal board of directors, neither should you. As you embark upon your journey with a decided heart, I can promise you the clamor from your personal peanut gallery of doubters and not-so-well-wishers will roar. It will amaze you! The people you thought would be on your side—but aren't—might be a larger group than you imagined. If you worry about what other people think, you will have more confidence in their opinions than you do in your own. Your future does not depend on the opinions or the permission of others.

If you are afraid of criticism, you'll have little effect on the world. Criticism runs rampant, and if you're inhibited by it, you'll drown in its deep waters. Anytime you do something unrealistic by other people's standards, they'll be braying like donkeys.

IF YOU WORRY ABOUT WHAT OTHER PEOPLE
THINK, YOU WILL HAVE MORE CONFIDENCE IN
THEIR OPINIONS THAN YOU DO IN YOUR OWN.

Want to know why?

Sorry, I have no clue.

I've had this happen in my own life. I've seen it happen in the lives of friends and watched it as people worked to accomplish something great—and the critics come out of the woodwork. I don't know why people feel so threatened by their perception of your success that they manage to make you the focus of their lives. I do know, however, that you cannot let them become the focus of yours.

THE CORTÉS INITIATIVE

In 1519, an extraordinary man set sail on the final leg of a voyage from the shores of Cuba to the Yucatán Peninsula. On eleven ships, five hundred soldiers, one hundred sailors, and sixteen horses. The mission was clear: to take the world's richest treasure! It was a treasure of gold, silver, artifacts, and jewels. It had been held by the same army for six hundred years. This treasure was not a secret. The world knew about this treasure because army after army had tried to take it. Conqueror after conqueror had come with their forces to take this treasure, but nobody had been able to do it. Not for six hundred years!

Hernán Cortés was a conqueror. Today this occupation would be politically incorrect, but back then it was simply a job description. Doctors, bakers, conquerors . . . you get the idea.

MOST PEOPLE FAIL AT WHATEVER THEY ATTEMPT
BECAUSE OF AN UNDECIDED HEART. SUCCESS
REQUIRES THE EMOTIONAL BALANCE OF A
COMMITTED HEART. WHEN CONFRONTED WITH
A CHALLENGE, THE COMMITTED HEART WILL
SEARCH FOR A SOLUTION. THE UNDECIDED
HEART SEARCHES FOR AN ESCAPE.

Cortés was aware of the many conquerors who had attempted to claim this treasure and failed. But his approach was different. He gathered an army committed beyond the level of the common man. Rather than signing up every recruit that applied, Cortés interviewed first. He talked to them about the treasure, what their lives would be like when they took the treasure, and what their families' and future generations' lives would be like when they took the treasure. He even fantasized about what it would be like the moment they put their hands on the treasure. He sold the people on the vision. They committed and set sail.

Halfway through the voyage, Cortés had a problem. Many of the soldiers and sailors who were once "so certain" turned into whiners: "Mr. Cortés . . . we're not sure we should be on this ship at this time." Or "This isn't what we expected it to be . . ."

When they arrived at the Yucatán Peninsula, Cortés gathered everybody on the beach. They grew quiet, waiting for Cortés to say, "You go here, we'll go there. If the arrows start flying, meet me at this coconut stump . . . we're out of here."

Instead, he leaned in and said, "Burn the boats."

"Excuse me?!" they replied incredulously.

Cortés repeated, "Burn the boats. Torch the boats."

"If we go home," he added, "we're going home in *their* boats." And on their leader's orders, *they burned their own boats*!

And an amazing thing happened. They fought really well. For the first time in six hundred years—the treasure was taken!

Why? Because their choice was to take the treasure . . . or die!

Burning Our Boats

The question for you is simple: *What boats in your mind continue to float the excuses and limiting beliefs that are keeping you from getting what you say you want? What boats in your life do you need to burn?*

Most of us are scared to burn boats because we know we'll get criticized if we do. Have you ever been criticized for something you believed or for something you've done with good intentions or because you're different? Doesn't it hurt? It's a horrible feeling.

Do you want to find out right now how to overcome criticism and that awful feeling of being criticized?

There are some people in your life who are never going to like you. Some people won't like anything you do as you become more successful. Think about your favorite book or movie of all time. Now go online and start reading consumer reviews on Amazon .com or some other product review website. It doesn't matter if your favorite book has sold more than twenty million copies or if your favorite movie did over $500 million at the box office, you'll find plenty of critical reviews.

I was wondering the other day, *Does anybody in the world get a pass? Is there anybody in the world that everybody likes?*

That very evening I heard someone on a talk show say, "And that's just another example of the Oprah-fication of America!"

It was obvious the term was being used to imply, "I don't like her."

Many might ask, "How can you not like Oprah? This nice, wonderful woman who does good things around the world? She's generous, kindhearted, smart, funny . . . How can you not like her?

But many don't.

The Catholic Church finished the beatification for both Mother Teresa and Pope John Paul II, declaring them saints. As part of the process, people argue against their sainthood. And what do they say? I have no clue. What could they say? But these critics do show up.

When we are bothered by criticism, what we most need is a good dose of perspective. So here is ours. Folks, the critics are bad-mouthing Oprah and Mother Teresa! Who are we to be exempt? We must accept it for what it is . . . the babbling of rabble that ultimately cannot help you or do harm. Ignore them.

UNLOCKING YOUR HIDDEN DREAM

If you had one hidden dream, secretly nursed close to your heart, what would it be? In your journal describe it in great detail.

THRIVING ON REJECTION

The fact is that criticism and rejection hurt, but you must shield yourself from them to protect your decided heart. Let me tell you what I do to protect my decided heart. When I was working on getting *The Traveler's Gift* published, the book kept getting turned down. I received a note from the top literary agent at William Morris. He wrote, "I found your story a bit melodramatic and lacking in concrete plot and characterization. Also, I didn't feel the characters you describe come to life."

Okay, so you don't like the story, I thought. *You don't like the plot or the characterization. And you don't like the characters. Other than that, what didn't you like?*

CRITICISM, CONDEMNATION, AND COMPLAINT
ARE CREATURES OF THE WIND. THEY COME
AND GO ON THE WASTED BREATH OF LESSER
BEINGS AND HAVE NO POWER OVER ME.

My little trick to keep my decided heart thriving, happy, and moving on the road toward my assured destiny during this trying time was to find other authors I admired who received this same kind of rejection.

I actually felt pretty good after I found a rejection letter of *The Diary of Anne Frank*. The publisher said, "This girl doesn't have any special perception or feeling that would lift that book above the curiosity level." More than twenty-five million copies of *The Diary of Anne Frank* have been sold worldwide.

When the manuscript for the classic *Lord of the Flies* was submitted, the publisher commented, "It does not seem to me that you've been wholly successful in working out this idea." More than 14.5 million copies have sold to date.

An unknown writer called Dr. Seuss presented a publisher with a manuscript titled *And to Think That I Saw It on Mulberry Street*. The manuscript was rejected by twenty-seven publishers, including one who said, "This is too different from the other books for juveniles on the market to warrant its selling. We pass."

Most of us read George Orwell's classic *Animal Farm* in school. The publisher said, "It is impossible to sell animal stories in the United States." *Animal Farm* has sold more than ten million copies.

I really felt I was in good company when I read the rejection letter sent to Rudyard Kipling for a manuscript he submitted titled *The Jungle Book*. The publisher sent back this note: "I'm sorry, Mr. Kipling, but you just don't know how to use the English language." I thought, *Holy cow. I'm in good company.*

That's what I do to protect my decided heart.

ELIMINATING DEBILITATING BELIEFS

Some of the greatest challenges to having a decided heart are our conscious and unconscious limiting beliefs. These limiting beliefs often translate into negative self-talk, such as, *I can't do it, I'm not good enough, I'm not smart enough,* or *I can't make it work.*

Many of these debilitating beliefs are hidden safely away from our conscious mind. They remain destructive to our growth until they are uncovered and understood, dismantled, and released. Often, simply becoming conscious of the limiting beliefs can help dissolve them.

What are five limiting beliefs you have about yourself? Think back to the fears you defined in the Overcoming

Fear exercise on page 55. Behind every fear is at least one debilitating belief about yourself. Uncover your destructive beliefs and write them down.

The Passion of Decisiveness

We're journeying toward a destiny that is assured because we have decided hearts. People such as Michael Jordan, Oprah Winfrey, Albert Einstein, Richard Branson, and Tiger Woods are so extraordinary because they have mastered life on their own terms, with decided hearts. With decided hearts, we learn to defy conventional standards with a childlike playfulness. We can actually develop a sense of excitement that triggers action in the face of criticism and rejection, breeding solutions and movement toward what we want instead of what we don't want. It awakens a burning desire and relentless determination when the odds are stacked against us.

POOR IS THE MAN WHOSE FUTURE DEPENDS ON
THE OPINIONS AND PERMISSION OF OTHERS.
REMEMBER THIS: IF YOU ARE AFRAID OF
CRITICISM, YOU WILL DIE DOING NOTHING!

Distilled into one word, the idea of a decided heart *is passion*. Passion comes from the heart. It has nothing to do with the mind. In fact, in times of decision, you might have heard somebody say, "The whole thing moved from my head to my heart." That's passion. Passion assists you when you have a great dream. It breeds conviction and turns mediocrity into excellence in everything you do.

Passion inspires other people to join you in your pursuit. You can set yourself on fire and people will come to watch you burn.

Passion helps you overcome insurmountable obstacles. You become unstoppable! Your life becomes a statement—an example. Others will see their futures in your eyes.

Joan of Arc was only seventeen when she led the armies of France against the English. One afternoon as the armies of France were approaching the city, they saw in the distance tens of thousands of soldiers manning the barricades at every elevation. Joan of Arc told her leaders, "Immediately. Now. Now, we must take them. Now." The leaders were horrified at her boldness and passion for winning this battle against seasoned warriors! After all, she was a peasant girl leading a rabble of men from France.

"I intend to strike at the heart of the barricade," she said.

"If you go in, not a man will follow you," they told her.

Simply, she replied, "I won't be looking back."

This young girl's passion changed history. What can you do with the passion in your heart?

ARCHITECTING THE GREATEST SHOW ON EARTH

Phineas Taylor Barnum was born one day late, July 5, 1810. He would have preferred fireworks and a celebration coast to coast to commemorate the arrival of the Greatest Showman on Earth. But, as nature would have it, he missed the party by four hours. The name Phineas was well placed. Its biblical meaning is "brazen mouth." P. T.'s maternal grandfather had the most influence on the boy in his formative years. The bespectacled, mop-headed, boisterous old man dearly loved his grandson and spent much of his time pulling one over on him. In P. T.'s own words, "My grandfather would go farther, wail longer, work harder, and contrive deeper to carry out a practical joke than for anything else under heaven." This model served Phineas well in his later years.

His father died when he was fifteen, leaving the family bankrupt and Phineas as the sole supporter. Phineas worked as a clerk in a nearby general store (of which he owned half), where he discovered his ability for promotion and vision. And in July 1835, Barnum's destiny came calling. A man named Coley Bartram walked into the store and spoke of a woman called Joice Heth, who was allegedly 161 years old and the nursemaid of President George Washington during his infancy. The man currently in charge of the Joice Heth Show was eager to return to his home state of Tennessee and was looking for a buyer for the show.

Barnum was hungry for a bigger and better opportunity. They haggled over the three-thousand-dollar asking price, agreeing on one thousand dollars for the Joice Heth Show. To secure the purchase, Barnum talked the seller into a purchase-option arrangement for five hundred. Five hundred dollars was all the money Barnum had in the world, but he was certain he had made the right decision. Barnum sold his partner his half of the grocery store to get the money, and in a few short days, Barnum went from store clerk to showman.

Careful planning, staging, and promotion turned this 161-year-old woman of exceptional mind and wit into a small industry. Then the inevitable happened: Joice Heth went on to meet her Maker. True to his word, Barnum allowed a famous surgeon friend to perform a postmortem examination. Dr. David L. Rogers returned findings that shocked and frightened Barnum: Joice Heth was no more than eighty years of age at the time of her death. The scandal hit the paper with the headline: "HOAX!"

Barnum was devastated. He had done his research and was convinced that Heth's records were authentic. Barnum's decided heart began to waver. Although he knew his destiny, he feared this controversy marked the end of his career.

What actually happened was astounding. As the allegations

flew and the story grew, a strange promotional phenomenon was born. The suspected hoax became a part of the promotional fabric of the Joice Heth story, actually increasing the value of the show. Once Barnum recognized what was happening, he moved the excitement and conflict of Joice's story into other shows that attracted huge paying crowds bent on figuring out their authenticity. Jumbo the Elephant, the mermaid from Fiji, the Cardiff Giant, the original Siamese Twins, and others—some real, some unreal, and all fun—were born out of the Joice Heth "hoax." P. T. Barnum became known as "the Greatest Showman on Earth" as he put together tour after tour featuring oddities from around the world.

In 1881, he joined with rival showman James Anthony Bailey to found the famous Barnum & Bailey Circus and change entertainment forever. World famous for removing social barriers against entertainment and using curiosity and sensation in promotion, Barnum was indeed the greatest showman on earth. He was one of the first American entrepreneurs to realize the moneymaking potential of publicity.

Barnum learned from this Joice Heth experience to always move with a decided heart. He learned that even when things look hopeless, our belief doesn't have to align with the outward manifestation. Barnum most likely learned to manage his emotions carefully. Fear, dread, shame, and guilt can be piercing weapons against a decided heart. In Barnum's case they nearly blinded him from the opportunity that led to the creation of the modern circus.

What if he had followed his initial shameful emotions out of town? What if he'd been frightened into another career? He might have died a store clerk in a small Midwestern town. That's nothing to be ashamed of, but it's certainly not the exciting life that was to be P. T. Barnum's.

LIVING A LIFE OF UNLIMITED POSSIBILITY

With a decided heart, grab hold of your dream for your life, your family, and your future. Don't make choices based on facts or percentages—they'll always discourage you. I feel sad for the people who consider themselves "realistic." They live their lives according to *what is*. Please throw *what is* out the window. Forget *what is*.

Let's start living life with *what if*. What if life could be exactly as you choose? What if your heart is so powerful it creates the time you want with your children? What if you could be a full-time mom or dad? What if you could have all the kids' college education money saved up before they are freshmen? What if you could live without a house payment—with your mortgage paid in full?

If you could choose a perfect day, what would it look like? How early would you get up? How late would you sleep? Who would you choose to be around? And where on earth would you be?

ALL MY PROBLEMS BECOME SMALLER WHEN I
CONFRONT THEM. IF I TOUCH A THISTLE WITH
CAUTION, IT WILL PRICK ME, BUT IF I GRASP
IT BOLDLY, ITS SPINES CRUMBLE INTO DUST.

The Certain Decision reminds us: you have the power to choose how you live your life because you have a decided heart and your destiny is assured. Choose wisely, and remember, most people fail because of an undecided heart. That is not you. Determine that you have a decided heart, and your success will require the emotional fortitude of that decided heart.

When confronted with a challenge, a decided heart searches

for a solution—it is only the undecided heart that searches for an escape. You can't afford to wait for conditions to be exactly right. Why not? Because conditions are never exactly right!

You have vision for a reason. Your dream for your life and your family's is in your heart for a reason. That passion is a part of you. So, go! Proceed! Don't ask permission anymore. Take it! Go!

To wait, to wonder, to doubt, or to be indecisive is to deny the world of who you are and who you will become.

You have a decided heart, and your destiny is assured.

ARCHITECTING A NEW SELF-IMAGE

The five beliefs you highlighted earlier represent the major blocks to your decided heart. It's time to dismantle these negative beliefs and replace them with uplifting ones.

1. For each negative belief, determine its polar opposite. If you have a negative belief that says, "I'm too old to be creative and inventive," you might change it to, "My age gives me the wisdom and gift of creativity and invention."
2. Write down a new, positively stated belief for each negative one.

Recite these new statements as positive affirmations over the next thirty days. Through continual repetition of your affirmations, you'll reprogram your subconscious mind with your new beliefs (and erase the conflicting old ones).

REAL TRAVELER PROFILE: GENERAL
NORMAN SCHWARZKOPF

When someone mentions the word *leaders*, it's easy to think of General Norman Schwarzkopf. General Schwarzkopf was the commander of Allied Forces in Operation Desert Shield and Operation Desert Storm, and quite possibly the most popular American military figure of the past century. His strong and decisive leadership during the Gulf War helped bring an early end to that first conflict.

History will long remember the skill with which Schwarzkopf coordinated a war effort in a country deeply suspicious of foreigners, all the while maintaining the secrecy so critical to the success of our troops—not an easy task during America's first internationally televised war.

It seemed appropriate for General Schwarzkopf to represent the Certain Decision. Here's a personal correspondence from the general.

Dear Andy,

When I received your invitation to share a time of discouragement in my life, my immediate concern was how to select only one. The years have presented me with a series of crossroads which have often taken me down a different path than I might have chosen.

It is, of course, understood that if this were a perfect world, I would not be writing this letter at all. My childhood would have been easy, my military career without detours, and there would simply be no story to tell. As you know, that is not the case.

In December 1972, the Army was considering officers in my year group for early promotion to full colonel. Routine promotions were in order two years down the road, but after having gotten feelers from various generals who wanted me for a colonel's job, I thought I had a pretty good chance. No one had a right to expect an early promotion; however, being promoted early boosted an officer's reputation, and I'd secretly let myself look forward to it.

As I walked into the War College on a Monday morning in January, I saw several of my peers patting themselves on the back. At that moment, I knew my name was not on the list. I realized that I would have another shot at early promotion the following winter, but this was the first time in my career when I was clearly no longer at the front of the pack. Friends offered condolences, which made me feel worse, as well as theories as to why I had been bypassed. I was disappointed, confused, and shaken.

The following November, I was nominated by the Army to serve as a military aide to Vice President Gerald Ford. I was honored and excited to be chosen out of all the lieutenant colonels in the Army. This was a prestigious job that would leave me with powerful connections in the event I decided to retire.

As the selection process went on, I got my hopes up. I was interviewed by the Vice President's assistant for national security affairs and even sat down with the Vice President himself. I thought we really hit it off.

In early January 1974, two events happened almost simultaneously. First, the Army released its list for early promotion to colonel and, to my shock, again I'd not been selected. Then, a few days later, I was called and told I had not been selected to work with Gerald Ford. In addition to the discouragement I felt, my frustration level was at an all time high.

At this point, I must tell you two of the most important lessons I learned from those and other challenges I have faced: (1) don't dwell on disappointment—determine to do your best anyway, and (2) we don't always know what's best.

Moving forward, I was soon commanding troops as a colonel

in Alaska. This led to a troop command at Ft. Lewis, Washington, and promotion to brigadier general, followed by Pacific Command in Hawaii, and an assignment as assistant division commander of the 8th Mechanized Infantry—part of NATO's front-line defense in Germany.

After several other exciting assignments through the years, including command of the 24th Mechanized Infantry Division and participation in the Grenada student rescue operation, I took over Central Command headquartered in Tampa, Florida. My area of responsibility was the Middle East.

Looking back at my military career, I can see now that every struggle I endured pointed me toward my destiny in the Gulf War. The challenges we face in certain situations sometimes hold a purpose beyond our understanding at the time. We don't always know what's best. The tough times in my life often dealt with being put in positions not of my choosing, but the ultimate result is now a matter of history.

I am frequently asked if I miss the Army. I suppose the answer would have to be yes, but what I miss the most is the camaraderie of those who have suffered great adversity. This is the bond that links all old soldiers. Not surprisingly, it is also the bond that links successful people. Success without adversity is not only empty . . . it is not possible.

Sincerely,

H. Norman Schwarzkopf,
General, U.S. Army

FIVE

THE JOYFUL DECISION

TODAY I WILL CHOOSE TO BE HAPPY.

Our very lives are fashioned by choice. First we
make choices. Then our choices make us.

The Joyful Decision, when fully understood, becomes a
powerful catalyst for change in your life. Happiness is a
choice. This Decision can liberate your spirit with the
infinite joy available in each moment of every day.

TODAY I WILL CHOOSE TO BE HAPPY.

Beginning this very moment, I am a happy person, for I now truly understand the concept of happiness. Few others before me have been able to grasp the truth of the physical law that enables one to live happily every day. I know now that happiness is not an emotional phantom floating in and out of my life. Happiness is a choice. Happiness is the end result of certain thoughts and activities, which actually bring about a chemical reaction in my body. This reaction results in a euphoria, which, while elusive to some, is totally under my control.

Today I will choose to be happy. I will greet each day with laughter.

Within moments of awakening, I will laugh for seven seconds. After even such a small period of time, excitement has begun to flow through my bloodstream. I feel different. I am different! I am enthusiastic about the day. I am alert to its possibilities. I am happy!

Laughter is an outward expression of enthusiasm, and I know that enthusiasm is the fuel that moves the world. I laugh throughout the day. I laugh while I am alone, and I laugh in conversation with others. People are drawn to me because I have laughter in my heart. The world belongs to the enthusiastic, for people will follow them anywhere!

Today I will choose to be happy. I will smile at every person I meet.

My smile has become my calling card. It is, after all, the

most potent weapon I possess. My smile has the strength to forge bonds, break ice, and calm storms. I will use my smile constantly. Because of my smile, the people with whom I come in contact on a daily basis will choose to further my causes and follow my leadership. I will always smile first. That particular display of a good attitude will tell others what I expect in return.

My smile is the key to my emotional makeup. A wise man once said, "I do not sing because I am happy; I am happy because I sing!" When I choose to smile, I become the master of my emotions.

Discouragement, despair, frustration, and fear will always wither when confronted by my smile. The power of who I am is displayed when I smile.

Today I will choose to be happy. I am the possessor of a grateful spirit.

In the past, I have found discouragement in particular situations, until I compared the condition of my life to others less fortunate. Just as a fresh breeze cleans smoke from the air, so does a grateful spirit remove the cloud of despair. It is impossible for the seeds of depression to take root in a thankful heart.

My God has bestowed upon me many gifts, and for these I will remember to be grateful. Too many times I have offered up the prayers of a beggar, always asking for more and forgetting my thanks. I do not wish to be seen as a greedy child, unappreciative and disrespectful. I am grateful for sight and sound and breath. If ever in my life there is a pouring out of blessings beyond that, then I will be grateful for the miracle of abundance.

I will greet each day with laughter. I will smile at every person I meet. I am the possessor of a grateful spirit.

Today I will choose to be happy.

BEWARE OF CONDITIONING

The U.S. standard rail gauge—the distance between the two rails—is exactly four feet, eight and one-half inches. An odd number, but that's the way they built them in England, and it was the English expatriates who built the railroads in the United States.

So why did the English build their rails with such odd measurements? The same people who built the pre-railroad tramways built their rails with a gauge of four feet, eight and one-half inches.

And why did they build them like that? The tramways reused the same jig, tools, and measurements that had been used to build wagons, which used that same wheel spacing: four feet, eight and one-half inches.

And why did the wagons have that particularly odd wheel spacing? If the spacing had been different, the wagon wheels would've broken on some of the old, long-distance roads in England . . . which incidentally had wheel ruts with the same spacing.

So who built the old rutted roads? The Imperial Roman Empire built the first roads in England thousands of years ago, and these roads can still be walked on today. The ruts are spaced exactly four feet, eight and one-half inches apart, because the Roman war chariots made the initial ruts. And every one of them had to match, for fear of destroying their wagon wheels and wagons. Since the chariots were made for and by the Imperial Realm, they were all alike in their wheel spacing.

So the U.S. standard rail gauge of four feet, eight and one-half inches comes from the original specifications for an Imperial Roman war chariot.

This is a classic example of conditioning—people doing things because that's the way they've always been done. There are businesses in trouble today, headed for a cliff they don't see, because of how they've been conditioned—they were successful doing things a certain way in years past, and they don't see that the market has changed or that the way they're doing things is no longer productive or that they are out-of-date and out of style. They keep making decisions based on how things have always been done.

So next time you're handed some instructions or some idea and you wonder, *What horse's rear end came up with this?* you might be exactly right. You see, the Imperial Roman war chariots were made just wide enough, four feet, eight and one-half inches, to accommodate the back end of two warhorses!

Now here's an interesting twist to this story: When you see a space shuttle sitting on the launchpad at Cape Canaveral, you will notice two big booster rockets attached to the side of the main fuel tanks. These SRBs (solid rocket boosters) are manufactured by a company in Utah. The engineers who designed them may have preferred to make them a bit wider, but the SRBs had to be shipped by train from the factory site to the launch site. The railroad line from the factory had to run through a tunnel in the mountains, and the SRBs had to fit through that tunnel. The tunnel is slightly wider than the railroad tracks, and the railroad track at four feet, eight and one-half inches, is about as wide as two horses' rear ends. So, the major design feature of what is arguably the most advanced transportation system in the world was determined, literally, by the width of a horse's behind. Can you imagine?

A HAPPY CHOICE

When you consider the Joyful Decision, "Today I will choose to be happy," do you see why it's important to understand conditioning? The Joyful Decision has been conditioned *out* of most people. Most people don't realize happiness is a choice! They are doing the same things every day, just because that's the way they've always done it. They're waking up grumpy, going through the motions at work, sitting in traffic without a smile on their faces. Life is killing them.

The Joyful Decision is more controversial on its surface than any of the other Seven Decisions because people don't understand it. If you're looking for a key to increasing your financial portfolio, this is the Decision that will make you more money.

I was doing a radio interview about *The Traveler's Gift*, and I had a very cynical talk show host ask me about the Joyful Decision. He said, "I just have to tell you, I'm not into a lot of this personal growth stuff, but this one . . . this one really seems ridiculous to me."

I laughed and said, "Okay, tell me why."

COMPLAINING IS AN ACTIVITY JUST AS LISTENING
TO THE RADIO IS AN ACTIVITY. ONE MAY CHOOSE TO
TURN ON THE RADIO, AND ONE MAY CHOOSE NOT
TO TURN ON THE RADIO. ONE MAY CHOOSE TO
COMPLAIN, AND ONE MAY CHOOSE NOT TO
COMPLAIN. I CHOOSE NOT TO COMPLAIN.

He said, "Well, I understand why you would want to accept responsibility, and I understand why you would want to seek wisdom and be a person of action . . . I understand those decisions, but come on—in the economic climate that our country is in, with people out of work, how could choosing to be happy make a difference?"

I said, "You gotta be kidding me. Listen. Think about this: Consider yourself an employer. You have two prospective employees standing in front of you with the same educational background. They are basically the same age, have the same experience, and even look and dress the same. One of them gripes and complains, and the other one smiles and is happy.

"Who are you going to hire? Well, the happy one, of course, because that's the person you want to be around! Who wants to be around a complainer? And everyone else is just like you. They want to be around happy people too. And this is why, today, you must choose to be happy. It's the beginning of a new life!"

I urge you to choose to be happy. There are so many things about which we can choose to be happy! Happiness is not some emotional phantom floating in and out of your life. You can choose happiness every day. Laughter and enthusiasm are the fuels that move the world. The world belongs to the enthusiastic, and people will follow them anywhere.

DEVELOPING YOUR HAPPY TRIGGERS

List five things you can do each day to make yourself laugh and smile. What can you think about? Is there a scene from a movie that always makes you laugh? Did your child do something so innocent and precious that it brought a smile to your face? Does your dog chase his tail?

The point is there are "happy triggers" all around us, but if we don't actively seek them out, we may only accidentally trigger them on rare occasions. By consciously identifying happy triggers, you can choose to be happy whenever you wish.

A Possessor of a Grateful Spirit

Now, if the last few paragraphs have irritated you . . . calm down. I don't *really* believe you can choose to be happy, snap your fingers, and have the feeling immediately. That is a bit ridiculous. I do, however, know for a fact that measures of happiness will result from simply choosing to be grateful.

Happiness—true happiness, that is—comes from deep within. Happiness comes from a grateful heart. It is impossible to be ungrateful and happy at the same time. Depression, anger, resentment, and other lower emotions may arise, but a grateful spirit keeps you from feeling sorry for yourself—the seeds of depression cannot take root in a grateful heart.

Occasionally, people come up to me in an airport and say, "I've heard you speak, and you know, I'm just not a happy person."

I might respond with, "Well, a great exercise for becoming a happy person is to sit down with a piece of paper and a pen and list the things for which you're grateful."

Occasionally they will reply, "Well, I just really don't have anything in my life to be grateful for."

I'll cross my arms, lean in confidently, smile, and ask, "Where are you flying to today?"

They'll tell me, and I'll respond, "You know, there's a lot of people driving to that city. There are even some people who want to get to that city and can't get there at all. Nice to be able to fly, isn't it?"

The realization hits them. "Oh, yeah, it really is nice to be able to fly."

"You know, you live in the United States of America. Isn't it great to live in a country that so many people complain about?"

They'll frown. And I'll say, "For all the complaining people do about our country, it's nice to live in a place that has freedom of speech. And as bad as some people think it is, where else would you want to live?"

Think about it: You can be grateful for the taxes you pay—that means you are earning money. You can be grateful for the mess you have to clean up after a party because it means you were surrounded by friends. You can be grateful for the nice clothes you're wearing. I would imagine there are some people in the world who don't have any clothes at all. And if they fit a little too tightly, it means you have enough to eat!

> JUST AS A FRESH BREEZE CLEANS SMOKE
> FROM THE AIR, SO DOES A GRATEFUL SPIRIT
> REMOVE THE CLOUD OF DESPAIR. IT IS
> IMPOSSIBLE FOR THE SEEDS OF DEPRESSION
> TO TAKE ROOT IN A THANKFUL HEART.

Sometimes I smile and say, "Have you eaten lunch yet? Where do you eat in this airport?"

And they'll tell me where, or they'll say, "Well, I haven't had lunch yet."

"Did you eat before you got here? Did you eat yesterday?"

"Well, yeah."

"Wow. You ate. A lot of people in the world don't have that luxury. Aren't you grateful you have something to eat?"

You can be grateful for mowing your lawn. You can be grateful for the windows that need to be cleaned, the gutters that are stopped up, that lock you haven't gotten around to fixing. In fact, you can be grateful for all the things that are wrong with your house! Why? You have a house!

You can be grateful for the parking spot at the far end of that parking lot, because that means you can walk. And if you're in a wheelchair, can't you be grateful that you have one?

You can be grateful for a huge electric bill. There are a lot of people who are not able to be warm or cool when they want to be. You can be grateful for aching muscles at the end of the day. You're able to work. And you can be so grateful for that loud alarm clock that goes off before daylight every morning. If you heard it, it means you're alive.

When I went to Mexico City for World Vision International, for a couple of days they walked me around a slum where a million people lived. I'd known there were poor people in the world, but I'd never seen a million of them in one place! I saw my own children in the eyes of the children who were playing there amid broken glass and dead animals. It was horrible to see what they had to do to get water and food.

You want something to be grateful for? Walk into your bathroom, turn on the faucet, and watch that clean water come out. Let it run over your hand. As long as you want that clean water, it's available in your own bathroom, from your own faucet. We're pouring this clean water on our lawns and washing our cars and dogs . . . yet there are a million people in Mexico City who don't have clean water to drink. The water is brought into the neighborhoods with trucks, and the people carry it home in pots, pans, and plastic bags.

I want to urge you to condition yourself, on a daily basis, to find things to be grateful for. *Become the possessor of a grateful spirit.*

From this moment on, you will ignore the conditioning that has pervaded your life to this point. *You will ignore the conditioning that says you must wake up with a scowl on your face. You will ignore the conditioning that says children who laugh in a restaurant get on your nerves. You are creating new conditioning!*

You are the possessor of a grateful spirit. You are grateful for the laughter of children, for situations that make you struggle and make you stronger. You are grateful for the ability to find your way out, because you will be able to lead others out. *You are a leader.* Your conditioning from this point on says, *Today I will choose to be happy.*

CULTIVATING A GRATEFUL SPIRIT

You can be grateful about anything: being alive, the ability to breathe, the trees, the air, the sun, the stars, indoor plumbing, abundant food, the country in which you were born, your family, your friends, your pet, music, love, romance, a great movie, your favorite book, the clouds, the mountains, a flower, a child's laugh, a puppy's curiosity, a new idea, the telephone, the Internet, paintings, sculptures, plays, heating and air conditioning. Get the idea?

Make a list of at least one hundred things for which you are grateful. Extra credit for extending your list to two hundred!

WHO'S PACKING YOUR PARACHUTE?

To condition yourself to be happy, you must possess a grateful spirit. Learn how to express gratitude. Expressing gratitude magnifies our happiness and brings us more happiness.

I DO NOT DENY THE REALITY OF MY SITUATION. I DENY THE FINALITY OF IT. THIS, TOO, SHALL PASS.

Most people don't get thanked. There are so many invisible people running in and out of our lives, providing services we take for granted, and they never get thanked. When you stop and say,

"Hey! Just wanted to say thanks for what you're doing," the look on their faces will make you happy! It's easier to be happy when you are sharing happiness and gratitude.

Charles Plumb was a United States Navy jet pilot in Vietnam. On his seventy-sixth combat mission, his plane was hit by a surface-to-air missile. He ejected and floated down into enemy hands. Captured, he spent the next six years in a Vietnamese prison. He survived and now lectures on lessons he learned from that experience. One day, he and his wife were sitting in a restaurant, and a man at another table came up and said excitedly, "You're Plumb! You're Charles Plumb! You flew jet fighters into Vietnam from the aircraft carrier *Kitty Hawk*. You were shot down." He went on to reveal other details of the mission.

Plumb didn't recognize the man, so he asked, "How in the world did you know all that?"

The man replied, "I packed your parachute. I was in the navy too. I worked on the *Kitty Hawk*."

Charles Plumb couldn't believe it. He thanked the man for packing his parachute so many years ago. The man shook his hand and said, "Wow, I guess it worked."

Charles Plumb assured him, "It sure did. If your chute hadn't worked, I wouldn't be here today."

Plumb couldn't sleep that night—he kept thinking about that man. "I kept wondering what he had looked like in a navy uniform," he recalls. "White hat, a bib in the back, bell-bottom trousers. I wondered how many times I might have ignored him, not even acknowledged him with a 'Good morning, how are you?' You see, I was a fighter pilot. And he was just a sailor."

Charles Plumb thought about how many hours this sailor spent at that long wooden table in the bowels of the *Kitty Hawk*, carefully weaving the shrouds and folding the silks of each chute, each time holding in his hands the fate of someone he didn't know.

Today Charles Plumb regularly asks people, "Who's packing your parachute?" Everyone relies on someone to make it through the day. There are so many people in our lives who are invisible to us, but they're packing our parachutes—mental, emotional, spiritual, and physical.

We need these parachutes; we need these people! Sometimes, in the midst of our challenges, it's easy to forget to express our gratitude to these people, to say, "Hello," or "Please," or "Thank you." Because we're so preoccupied, we don't congratulate each other or ask if anything difficult is happening in their lives. We don't compliment each other or commit random acts of kindness.

It's amazing how, when you condition yourself to have a grateful spirit, you will find yourself expressing gratitude and multiplying that feeling in your life. Stop your car beside the road when the garbage men are there, and just holler out the window, "Hey! I just want to tell you how much we appreciate you guys. I thought the other day, *What would our house look like after a few weeks if these men didn't show up?* We appreciate you!"

You'll stand out in a huge way because, I promise you, nobody else is thanking them. You can thank the person who reads your gas or electric meter and tell him how much you appreciate him walking through the heat or the cold to keep your home cool or warm. You can thank the UPS man or FedEx lady or the people who work behind the desk at the post office. Smile at the people behind the airline counters. Tell the kid collecting the shopping carts from your grocery store's parking lot how much you appreciate being able to pick up a cart inside instead of hunting one up from the lot.

The possessor of a grateful spirit who shares that gratitude with others is *conditioned* to be happy. He or she wakes up happy!

CAPTURING YOUR MOMENTS TO REMEMBER

As technology advances, we seem to have more demands on our time. In an effort to "keep up," we often forget to remember the joyous, fun, even miraculous moments that unfolded before our very eyes.

What are some of the incredible moments to remember you've had during the past week, month, or year? It could be a big event like a daughter's wedding, or a simple moment when you and your loved one shared a smile.

Capture ten of these moments right now to help cultivate a grateful spirit. (What if you did this exercise every week?)

THE MAGIC OF SMILING

I mentioned earlier that happy people make more money. How can choosing to be happy actually increase your financial portfolio? Why do happy people make more money? I'm amazed when I hear people say, "Oh, I'm having some hard times financially. We just never have good things happen to us. People never help us. Opportunities never come our way."

When someone mumbles, "People don't help me," I think to myself, *Of course they don't help you! They don't even want to be around you! Smile! Put some energy into your voice! Become somebody others want to be around.*

WHEN I CHOOSE TO SMILE, I BECOME THE
MASTER OF MY EMOTIONS. DISCOURAGEMENT,
DESPAIR, FRUSTRATION, AND FEAR WILL ALWAYS
WITHER WHEN CONFRONTED BY MY SMILE.

I believe opportunities come from our associations. Think about it—our opportunities, our encouragement, our information and knowledge are most likely to come from other people. If that's true (and it is . . .), then we *must* become people whom others want to be around.

People want to be around happy people—not whiners, moaners, and groaners. Happy people get more opportunities because opportunities come from people, and people are attracted by happy people. And obviously, opportunities often translate into financial success.

If you have to fake it initially, fake it! Nobody expects you to be happy every moment of every day. But you can choose to smile. Speak a little faster. Move. You will attract people and opportunities into your life when you become someone others want to be around.

Your smile is your calling card. It is the most potent weapon you have. With your smile, you can forge bonds, break ice, and calm storms. Use your smile constantly. The power of who you are is revealed when you smile.

THE SMILE EXERCISE

Smiles are contagious. Smiles affect your biochemistry. Smile for the next sixty seconds as you remember your favorite leisure activity. Why do you enjoy it? What

---

benefits do you gain by pursuing that passion? Feel your smile through your entire body, including your breathing. And if you're having trouble remembering something that makes you smile, here are a few possibilities: your pet, your child, a sunset, a vacation, laughing with a close friend, your favorite show—whatever works for you!

How do you feel? Care to smile for more than sixty seconds? Go for it!

THE SECRET TO LASTING SUCCESS

I'm about to reveal the biggest secret to the Joyful Decision. I don't talk or write about it much even though I've been asked the question many times. I've often considered what I would say if somebody ever brings me in to speak and says, "You've got one minute on stage. And this is the last minute you'll ever speak in your entire life. Tell them one thing that can change everything."

I've got the secret. Are you ready? It's going to blow your mind because it's so simple. You can learn it in a couple of days, and it will change everything.

> PEOPLE ARE DRAWN TO A PERSON WITH
> LAUGHTER IN HIS HEART. THE WORLD
> BELONGS TO THE ENTHUSIASTIC, FOR
> PEOPLE WILL FOLLOW THEM ANYWHERE!

Here's the secret: *smile while you talk*. I'm not saying, "Smile a lot," or "Smile at everyone you meet." I'm saying, "Smile while you talk!" Very few people do this. Watch. Even when people tell a joke, they don't usually smile until they get to the punch line. Most tell jokes with a serious expression furrowed in their brow, get to the punch line, and then laugh with everyone else. In everyday conversation, the vast majority of us speak to others with a serious or bland expression on our faces.

Learn to smile while you talk, and your life will be forever transformed. And if you throw in a little chuckle while you're talking, even better. Why will everything change? People cannot help but smile at somebody who smiles at them!

I do this all the time when I speak. I'll walk around the room as I'm talking and look people in the eye, nod, and smile. Soon I'll have fifty or sixty people nodding with me in unison, because when you nod and smile at them, they will smile and nod back.

You want people to join the church softball team? You want them to buy the house from you? You want them to sign the deal? You want them to be clients forever? You want them to contribute to a cause? *Learn to smile while you talk!*

The same positive results will transpire with your family. Your spouse, your kids, your neighbors—everybody will react to you differently when you smile as you talk.

For many years I toured as a comedian. I was not under any delusion that my material was the greatest in the world, yet I was very successful, due in large part to smiling while I talked. I was known for being able to connect with an audience immediately, and that was because I smiled when I talked. I would hear other comedians talking about dealing with hecklers. I never dealt with hecklers because I didn't have any—I was everybody's friend. People deal with and react to their friends in a totally different way. You can make friends instantly if you smile while you talk.

SMILE-WHILE-TALKING EXERCISE

To do this exercise, you'll need to look into a mirror, so go into the bathroom, the bedroom, or any private place with a mirror.

For the next five days, for five to ten minutes each day, practice smiling while you talk. Incrementally add each of the following:

- A little chuckle, so a slight laughter comes through your voice
- An eyebrow lift and open eyes
- A little nod
- A faster cadence to your speech

Once you feel comfortable talking this way, begin practicing it casually with other people. Of course, you don't have to tell them you're practicing; just smile, nod, slightly chuckle, talk faster, and lift your eyebrows. It will change the way you interact with people and transform the opportunities that you will attract.

THE JOY OF STUPIDITY

As you begin fully living the Seven Decisions and becoming the person you want to be, you can choose to bring laughter into the lives of others. You can quickly become the funny person everyone wants to be around. When I was a comedian, it took me a while to understand where humor came from so that I could write it consistently.

Humor is discovered by considering a series of questions. Probably the biggest question comedians use to discover humor is, "What is stupid about this?" You can apply this question to everyday situations with your buddies, associates, and family. You'll find laughter that most people only dream about because there is no shortage of stupidity out there.

On the counter lay a frozen package of Mark and Spencer Bread Pudding. The instructions included directions on how to heat it up in the microwave, a conventional oven, or a convection oven. In large letters at the bottom, it read: *Warning. Product will be hot after heating.*

What is stupid about this?

On the packaging for Rowenta irons, there is a little notice on the bottom right: *Do not iron clothes on body.* Hmm . . . that would save a little time.

> MY SMILE HAS BECOME MY CALLING CARD.
> IT IS, AFTER ALL, THE MOST POTENT WEAPON
> I POSSESS. MY SMILE HAS THE STRENGTH
> TO FORGE BONDS, BREAK ICE, AND CALM
> STORMS. I WILL USE MY SMILE CONSTANTLY.

The label on the sleep aid Nytol reads as follows: *Warning: May cause drowsiness.* And I'm taking this because . . .

A Sears hair dryer: *Do not use while sleeping.* Mm-hmm . . .

Swanson frozen dinners: *Number one serving suggestion: Defrost.* That's just a suggestion.

The directions on the box for Dial soap: *Use like regular soap.*

The box for Tesco's Tiramisu Dessert: *Do not turn dessert upside down.* And guess where that instruction is printed? That's right, on the bottom.

Most brands of Christmas lights: *For indoor or outdoor use only.* As opposed to what?

And my favorite, on a Japanese food processor we got for Christmas, it reads: *Not to be used for the other use.* So what is stupid about this?

You can come up with your own family comedy show. Just watch your kids; watch your parents. Remember what your parents used to say that you're saying now. I'm telling you, so many things will be funny.

We have two boys at home, and we have learned that when you hear a flush and the words "Uh-oh," it's already too late. When they were younger, we knew to always look in the oven before we turned it on. (Tonka trucks don't do well at 375 degrees.) We also know now that a G.I. Joe's boot will indeed pass through the digestive tract of a four-year-old. There are so many things that, if you just look around, you can laugh at and be happy. As parents, as kids, and as kids with parents, there are so many things we all say that are crazy and funny! As we relate them to each other and laugh at ourselves, life is more fun.

LIVING A DOG'S LIFE

We used to have a Dalmatian named Lucy. She was our "dog-daughter" for a long time until we had *real* children. Lucy was a part of the family and especially important to my wife. For years I watched how Polly treated her, and occasionally, it irritated me. I told her one day, "You know, sometimes I think you treat that dog better than you treat me."

But I couldn't help noticing how Lucy acted.

When Polly came into the house after a morning out, I'd often be on the phone. I might say, "Hi," or if it was an important call, I might say, "Shhh." Or if I was writing, we'd often say hello from across the room.

Lucy, on the other hand, reacted totally differently when Polly entered the room. Lucy would stand up and start wagging her tail as if to say, "Hey, it's my mom! I love you!" She would then walk over to Polly and lick her face. "Ooooh, ooh, kiss, kiss, kiss." (She did this even if Polly was just in the room five minutes earlier!)

It occurred to me that maybe if I treated my wife as well as the dog treated her, then maybe she would treat me as well as she treats the dog.

How do you treat people when they "enter the room"? Are they uplifted as they encounter you?

And while we're talking about it, how do *you* enter a room? Do you know people who brighten the room as soon as they walk through the door? Their presence alone puts a smile on people's faces. These rare souls focus their energy and attention on making others laugh and smile. They ask questions of people they meet and genuinely want to hear the answers. They take such an interest in others that others can't help but take an interest in them.

Most of us tend to lock ourselves in our own worlds. We're so focused on our own problems and challenges in life that we don't "see" the soul standing before us.

Next time you're in the checkout line at your local supermarket, notice that there is a real person on the other side of that counter, with his or her own problems, likes, dislikes, and beliefs. Look this person in the eye and connect with him or her. Wordlessly acknowledge him or her as another soul walking with us on the planet. What if you made it a point to try to make the cashier at the checkout or the waiter in a restaurant smile? How might focusing on sharing joy with someone you don't know positively affect your attitude and life experiences? Transform your world by acting like a dog!

REAL TRAVELER PROFILE: AMY GRANT

Music was always a part of this multiplatinum, multi-Grammy music star's life. Amy Grant was discovered as an artist while working part-time sweeping floors and demagnetizing tapes at a Nashville studio. Her foray into the music business helped birth contemporary Christian music, a category that didn't exist at the time.

Thirty-plus years and many gold and platinum albums later, Amy has shared her music around the world. Amy is a great embodiment of the Joyful Decision.

Dear Andy,

Back in the spring of 1978, I released my first album. I was seventeen years old and full of dreams. That summer, after my class graduated from high school, I left on my first promotional tour. One stop on that tour was a book and record store in Southern California. I was to sign autographs and sing for ninety minutes. My mother was with me and we were very excited. The manager of the store had sent out 1,200 engraved invitations for the occasion. Obviously, everyone involved was expecting a large crowd.

Well, the crowd never made it. In fact, not one single person showed up! . . . Oh well—the store manager listened to me sing for an hour and a half. He listened to me sing by himself because even my mother left. (I'm not kidding!) This probably still ranks as the single most "distinguishing" event of my career.

I can't say, without a doubt, that quitting didn't enter my mind that day, but I'm glad that I didn't. That experience (and several like it) gave me a deep appreciation for the support of a kind of audience that I might never have gained otherwise. Besides, the memory of that afternoon still makes me laugh inside, just as it did the last time I looked out from the stage of the Pacific Amphitheater in Southern California to 20,000 smiling faces.

I know that there are no guarantees in life. I also know that good things rarely come about the first time around. And so my advice would be: Whatever your goals—don't give up! More important than talent, strength, or knowledge is the ability to laugh at yourself and enjoy the pursuit of your dreams.

Sincerely,

Amy Grant

SIX

The Compassionate Decision

I WILL GREET THIS DAY WITH A FORGIVING SPIRIT.

Forgiveness is a secret that is hidden in plain sight. It costs nothing and is worth millions. It is available to everyone and used by few. If you harness the power of forgiveness, you will be sought after and regarded highly. And not coincidentally, you will also be forgiven by others!

The Compassionate Decision changes the way most people view forgiveness. A forgiving spirit allows you to let go of the past and embrace a compelling new future. Harboring anger and resentment for others—regardless of whether or not "they deserve it"—poisons your soul and limits your growth. When you embrace forgiveness through the Compassionate Decision, your level of personal success becomes boundless.

I WILL GREET THIS DAY WITH A FORGIVING SPIRIT.

For too long, every ounce of forgiveness I owned was locked away, hidden from view, waiting for me to bestow its precious presence upon some worthy person. Alas, I found most people to be singularly unworthy of my valuable forgiveness, and, since they never asked for any, I kept it all for myself. Now, the forgiveness that I hoarded has sprouted inside my heart like a crippled seed yielding bitter fruit.

No more! At this moment, my life has taken on new hope and assurance. Of the world's population, I am one of the few possessors of the secret to dissipating anger and resentment. I now understand that forgiveness only has value when it is given away. By the simple act of granting forgiveness, I release the demons of the past about which I can do nothing and create in myself a new heart, a new beginning.

I will greet this day with a forgiving spirit. I will forgive even those who do not ask for forgiveness.

Many are the times when I have seethed in anger at a word or deed thrown into my life by an unthinking or uncaring person. Valuable hours have been wasted imagining revenge or confrontation. Now I see the truth revealed about this psychological rock inside my shoe. The rage I nurture is often one-sided, for my offender seldom gives thought to his offense!

I will now and forevermore silently offer my forgiveness

even to those who do not see that they need it. By the act of forgiving, I am no longer consumed by unproductive thoughts. My bitterness is given up. I am contented in my soul and effective again with my fellow man.

I will greet this day with a forgiving spirit. I will forgive those who criticize me unjustly.

Knowing that slavery, in any form, is wrong, I also know that the person who lives a life according to the opinion of others is a slave. I am not a slave. I have chosen my own counsel. I know the difference between right and wrong. I know what is best for the future of my family, and neither misguided opinion nor unjust criticism will alter my course.

Those who are critical of my goals and dreams simply do not understand the higher purpose to which I have been called. Therefore, their scorn does not affect my attitude or action. I forgive their lack of vision and forge ahead. I now know that criticism is part of the price paid for leaping past mediocrity.

I will greet this day with a forgiving spirit. I will forgive myself.

For many years, my greatest enemy has been myself. Every mistake, every miscalculation, every stumble I made has been replayed over and over in my mind. Every broken promise, every day wasted, every goal not reached has compounded the disgust I feel for the lack of achievement in my life. My dismay has developed a paralyzing grip.

When I disappoint myself, I respond with inaction and become more disappointed.

I realize today that it is impossible to fight an enemy

living in my head. By forgiving myself, I erase the doubt, fear, and frustration that have kept my past in the present. From this day forward, my history will cease to control my destiny. I have forgiven myself. My life has just begun.

I will forgive even those who do not ask for forgiveness. I will forgive those who criticize me unjustly. I will forgive myself.

I will greet this day with a forgiving spirit.

THE ANGER-MANAGEMENT MYTH

Traditional wisdom tells us the most effective way of dealing with rage or resentment is a course in anger management. There are mental health professionals who deal exclusively in anger management. There are ads in the newspaper for anger-management courses at your local college. It is part of our cultural consciousness—an athlete does something crazy, and the team sends him to anger management.

In 2006, football's Tennessee Titans defensive lineman Albert Haynesworth stomped on the helmetless head of a Dallas Cowboys lineman after the play was over in an act of sheer rage at a blown play. His outburst required dozens of stitches and reconstructive surgery to the lineman's face. Albert humiliated his team, and the NFL reprimanded Albert with a five-game suspension and encouraged him to take an anger-management course.

We hear about celebrity court cases, with part of the sentence being an anger-management course. Fortune 500 executives often enroll staff members in anger-management courses. Jack Nicholson and Adam Sandler costarred in a movie titled *Anger Management*.

This traditional wisdom is horribly flawed. Think about the

term *anger management*: Why would you want to *manage* something like anger? Forget about managing anger; let's get rid of it. Anger *resolution* can be accomplished by utilizing the Compassionate Decision: "I will greet this day with a forgiving spirit." And, yes, my friend, before you even ask the question, it really is just that simple!

THE ULTIMATE ANGER-RESOLUTION COURSE

Forgiveness is the ultimate resolution of anger. For years, I thought forgiveness was something to hoard—something to be doled out on a case-by-case basis, determined by whether someone deserved it. It was like knighthood, bestowed upon the person who crawled into my presence, wailing and begging me for it. If I deemed him worthy, I would lay my sword upon his shoulder. "You are forgiven. Now depart from me."

Naturally, part of me thrived on that anger, and I held grudges for a long time. But as the grudges build, they can weigh us down. Eventually, we're so bogged down that we often can't remember who to forgive or the specifics of the original event. We become preoccupied by other people, and our lives become a catastrophic mess. By forgiving, we complete the ultimate course in anger resolution.

FORGIVENESS IS THE ULTIMATE
RESOLUTION OF ANGER.

I couldn't find a rule in any book I've ever read (including the Bible) that said in order for me to forgive somebody, the person who committed the offense had to ask for it or deserve it. And I couldn't find anything that said, "Well, you can forgive a person as long as he or she hasn't been doing the same stupid thing over and over again for twenty years."

Everything I read and everything I felt within my soul said,

"Forgive. Let it go." I see now that by forgiving, I'm giving myself the ultimate gift, because forgiveness affects me much more than it affects another. It's not even mandatory that the person I'm forgiving be aware of it. Forgiveness often means more to the forgiver than it does to the person being forgiven.

Sometimes when I'm talking about this, people say, "So . . . they're just going to get away with it? I'm supposed to just forgive and forget?"

No. I'm not suggesting that at all. Forgiveness is about *you*. Trust is about *them*. Forgiveness is about the past; trust is about the future. Do we forgive somebody who steals from us? Yes. Do we continue to do business with him? No.

Forgiveness is a decision, not an emotion. If we approach it through our emotions, our emotions inevitably drag us the other way. But if you will notice, emotions follow decisions. When we decide to forgive, our emotions follow along.

THE GIFT OF FORGIVENESS

How many times have you been trying to fall asleep at night, when suddenly your peaceful trance is interrupted, and your eyes pop open? You remember what that guy at work said to you or what he did to you, and you can't believe it! You keep replaying what happened over and over, thinking about what you should have said differently or what you might say tomorrow if you have the chance. And you think about punching him out. (That's correct, ladies. Forty- and fifty-year-old men still think like boys in the sandbox.) You're consumed in the middle of the night, wide-awake, thinking about this person.

Or perhaps you're driving along, and everything's fine. You're comfortable, having a great conversation with your family, when you remember something. Your spouse asks, "What's wrong?"

And you answer, "What do you mean, what's wrong?"

"Well, you just stopped talking. And you haven't said anything for five minutes."

You realize that you were thinking about that guy and what he said and what you wish you would have said.

FORGIVENESS IS ABOUT YOU. TRUST IS
ABOUT THEM. FORGIVENESS IS ABOUT THE
PAST; TRUST IS ABOUT THE FUTURE.

Here's the crazy thing: 99 percent of the time, the people we're so irritated and bent out of shape about, these bozos who have offended us so deeply, are sleeping peacefully in their beds or living their lives, absolutely without a clue that we are even thinking about them! Often, they're unaware they've done anything to offend us in the first place.

So if they're not going to ask forgiveness, and if it doesn't matter if they ask or not, and if it doesn't matter if they deserve it or not, and if it doesn't matter how many times they've done it, and if they're not even thinking about it, but it's ruining your life . . . why should you forgive them?

Because it's ruining your life, not theirs! Trust me on this! You cannot become the parent, spouse, or friend you could otherwise be while consumed by an unforgiving attitude.

Forgiveness is a gift you give yourself. Receive it now!

THE RESENTMENT DISCHARGE

Have you been harboring resentment toward anyone? Go back to when you were a kid and review your resentments:

who are the people who've imprisoned you through your resentment toward them?

Now close your eyes, and let go of your resentments for each person. Forgive them. Remember, your resentments only hurt yourself. Forgiving those toward whom you hold anger, resentment, or hatred liberates your spirit; life becomes infinitely more peaceful. To successfully complete this exercise, don't make any exceptions—forgive each person unconditionally (especially that one person you really don't want to forgive).

Commit from this day forward to embrace the Compassionate Decision of forgiveness unconditionally. We generally avoid unconditional forgiveness because of the secret payoff our egos get from harboring emotions like anger and resentment. Surrender the payoff of those "lesser" emotions, and embrace a new life filled with infinite freedom and joy!

THE MIRACLE OF FORGIVENESS

Do the names Jo Berry or Patrick Magee ring a bell for you? Probably not. Perhaps you remember the Brighton Bomb incident in 1984? The Irish Republican Army bombed the Grand Hotel in Brighton, England, in an attempt to kill Prime Minister Margaret Thatcher and her entire cabinet during a Tory Party conference.

Five people died in this enormous blast, including a gentleman by the name of Sir Anthony Berry, who left behind six children, including his daughter, Jo Berry. Patrick Magee was charged with planting and detonating the IRA device and was given eight life sentences by Justice Boreham.

How does a daughter who lost her father under such devastating circumstances go about healing the painful anger that swelled within her? Jo came to realize that she must "seek to understand, not condemn." As she explains, "I'm beginning to realize that no matter what side of the conflict you're on, had we all lived each other's lives, we all could have done what the other did."

Through empathy, compassion arises; with compassion, we are less likely to judge others. But how can we learn to empathize in the face of swelling anger and grief?

As Jo explains, "An *inner shift* is required to hear the story of the enemy. For me, the question is always about whether I can let go of my need to blame and open my heart enough to hear Pat's story and understand his motivations. The truth is that sometimes I can and sometimes I can't. It's a journey and it's a choice, which means it's not all sorted and put away in a box."

It's difficult to imagine what this must have been like for Jo Berry. Her father was killed unnecessarily by this act of violence, but somehow she held on to a hope that something positive would shine through this traumatic event. She went to Ireland and listened to the stories of courageous people who were entangled in the web of violence.

In 2000, Jo decided she wanted to have a face-to-face meeting with the person who took her father's life—she wanted to see Pat as a real human being rather than the enemy. Jo recalls, "At our first meeting, I was terrified, but I wanted to acknowledge the courage it had taken him to meet me. We talked with an extraordinary intensity. I shared a lot about my father, while Pat told me some of his story."

For more than two and a half years, Jo and Pat got to know each other. Each of them, it seems, is on a path toward recovering their humanity through forgiveness. Some might argue that a caring relationship between these two people under this difficult circumstance is nothing short of a miracle. Through the power of a forgiving spirit, the miraculous is possible.*

HOPE-FUL FORGIVENESS

Occasionally you're on the flip side of the coin—someone is angry at you. Something you said or did offended someone. Now the other person has the opportunity to forgive you. Assuming that person is aware of the Compassionate Decision, as you are, you must give him the opportunity to work through his anger. It can be challenging to humbly ask someone for forgiveness. But it works.

Asking for forgiveness is an amazing experience, and one that only truly extraordinary people will do. It's much easier to simply let stuff slide, especially if the issue involves someone you're not going to run into again or someone who doesn't, on the surface, matter that much to you. But if he or she is a human being, a person on this planet with you, he or she matters. It takes courage to walk up to someone and say, "Hey, I need to talk to you. I owe you an apology, and I want to ask for your forgiveness." Oftentimes your humility will create a bond or forge a new friendship that will benefit you in some way. This action almost always dissipates and resolves the anger.

When I was working with Bob Hope, he was very nice to me. This was a great man.

I was doing a television show one night, and the host said, "What's it like working with Bob Hope?"

And I replied, "Oh, he's great. He is just so fun and, you know, as old as he is, it's amazing how sharp he continues to be. He's incredible. I really like him."

It was brought to my attention a couple of days later that Mr.

---

* Andy interviews Jo Berry and Patrick Magee together. You can watch the video on AndyAndrews.com.

Hope was not very happy about my comment on his age. Now, I could have just dismissed it and said, "Well, holy cow. You know, if he doesn't know he's old . . ." But here is a guy who had been very kind to me. I valued his friendship. I could not get it out of my mind that I had offended him. What I had done wasn't malicious or even harmful, but I said something that hurt his feelings. At that point, his feelings were much more important than my own. I kept thinking about it, and my wife said, "Well, if you're so concerned about it, you just need to call him."

I thought, *I'm not calling Bob Hope at his house.*

She said again, "You need to call."

OFTENTIMES YOUR HUMILITY WILL CREATE A
BOND OR FORGE A NEW FRIENDSHIP THAT WILL
BENEFIT YOU IN SOME WAY. THIS ACTION ALMOST
ALWAYS DISSIPATES AND RESOLVES THE ANGER.

So I did. I called Mr. Hope. The phone rang, and Mrs. Hope answered the phone. "Hi, Mrs. Hope. This is Andy Andrews. How are you doing?" We talked for a few minutes, and I asked, "Is your husband home?" He was.

Mr. Hope came to the phone. "Hi, Mr. Hope. This is Andy. Did I catch you at an okay time?"

"Yeah."

"Okay. Uh . . ." and I forged ahead. "You know, I was doing a television show the other night, and I don't know if this is accurate or not, but someone told me you were upset at something that I said on the show about your age."

And he said, "Yeah."

My heart sank. It was true.

"Mr. Hope," I began, "I deeply apologize. I am so sorry. I did not mean that maliciously, but I can understand how you would not have wanted me to say that, and I am so sorry that I did. I will watch myself in the future. I don't know what to do other than to ask you to forgive me. I truly value your friendship and our relationship. Would you please forgive me for doing that?"

The whole thing just melted. He said, "Of course, Andy. Don't worry about it. Man, if anybody understands saying something on television that you want to take back, it's me, so don't even worry about it. It's all forgotten."

He was absolutely terrific about it. It was one of the hardest things I've ever had to do. And now, since he's gone, I am so grateful that I didn't just apologize or say, "I'm sorry." Rather, I specifically asked for his forgiveness. And he gave it to me. I never have to feel bad about that again. Every time I think about Mr. Hope, I have good memories, and there's not even one little nagging, nit-picking thing in there. That's the power of forgiveness. It is resolution, not anger management. It erases the anger, gets rid of it completely.

A Powerful Act of Forgiveness

Remember the incredible story of Joshua Chamberlain in chapter 3? As I researched Abraham Lincoln for *The Traveler's Gift*, I discovered a thrilling connection between Lincoln and Chamberlain. When Lincoln went back to Washington after making the Gettysburg Address, he began to follow Joshua Chamberlain's career. Following the incredible underdog victory earlier in the war, Chamberlain actually led successful campaigns until the end of the war and was cited by the government four separate times for bravery in action. He was promoted to brigadier general for heroism at Petersburg, and a few months later he was cited for heroism at Five Forks and promoted to major general. At the end of the war, President Lincoln chose Joshua Chamberlain above all the Union officers to have the honor of accepting the Confederate surrender at Appomattox.

BY THE SIMPLE ACT OF GRANTING FORGIVENESS,
I RELEASE THE DEMONS OF THE PAST ABOUT
WHICH I CAN DO NOTHING AND CREATE IN
MYSELF A NEW HEART, A NEW BEGINNING.

There Chamberlain stunned the world with a show of forgiveness and respect: he ordered his troops to attention, saluting General Robert E. Lee and the defeated South. With that bold stroke, planned behind the scenes by Lincoln, of course, the president of the once-again United States of America began the healing of a nation and its people.

HEALING A WOUNDED HEART

With a pen and journal in hand, answer the following questions and jot down any names that come to mind during this exercise. When you're finished, review each name. Ask yourself, "Is this a person I need to forgive, or is this a person from whom I need to ask forgiveness?"

Notice the quality of these questions. Too many people ask unconstructive questions, such as, "What's wrong? Why is this happening to me?" Remember, the quality of your answers is determined by the quality of your questions. Ask quality questions—questions that make you think—and you'll get quality answers.

Here is a list of questions you may ask yourself:

- What one decision would I make if I knew it would not fail?
- What one thing should I eliminate from my life

because it holds me back from reaching my full potential?

- Am I on the path to something absolutely fantastic or something absolutely average?
- Am I running from something?
- How can I use my time better?
- What impossible thing am I believing and planning for?
- What is my most prevailing thought?
- What good thing have I committed myself to do that I've quit doing?
- Of the people I respect the most, what is it about them that earns my respect?
- What would a truly creative person do in my situation?
- What outside influences are causing me to be better? Worse?
- What gifts, talents, or strengths do I have?
- I know I don't have the answer right now, but if I knew the answer, what would I say?
- What is one thing I can do for someone else who has no opportunity to repay me?
- Who do I need to forgive?
- From whom do I need to ask forgiveness?

THE POISON OF UNFORGIVENESS

In his classic book *An Enemy Called Average*, John Mason wrote, "When faced with the decision to forgive and forget, never make the excuse, 'But no one knows what that person did to me!' That may be true," he said, "but the question is: do you know what unforgiveness will do to you?"

What *does* unforgiveness do to us? Have you ever experienced the mental illusion that life has you cornered? Have you ever felt boxed in, discouraged, controlled by outside circumstances? When I have felt that way in my own life, I've determined over the years that there is generally someone I haven't forgiven or someone from whom I haven't asked forgiveness. The person's name sticks in the back of my mind, as if it's subconsciously tapping me on the shoulder, diverting my focus from where it should be.

There is a story an old Indian man tells his grandson about a fight going on inside between two wolves. One wolf was evil and full of anger, envy, sorrow, regret, greed, arrogance, self-pity, guilt, resentment, inferiority, lies, false pride, and ego. And the other wolf was a good wolf, full of forgiveness.

> IN ORDER TO BE SUCCESSFUL IN ALL AREAS
> OF MY LIFE, I MUST CONTROL MY IMPULSES—
> MY THOUGHTS. IT IS IMPOSSIBLE TO FIGHT
> AN ENEMY THAT HAS A FORT IN MY HEAD.

The grandson asked his grandfather, "Which wolf wins?"

The old man simply replied, "The one I feed."

Most likely, as you read these words, there is a fight going on inside you between those same two wolves. The fight is revealing itself to you as someone's name or a visual image of that face. You can kill the wolf that contains all that anger, sorrow, regret, and resentment by embracing the good wolf and choosing forgiveness.

There is one person you need to forgive that if you don't, your effectiveness as a husband, as a wife, as a mother or father, as a friend or a leader will suffer. The key to bringing your dreams into reality is forgiveness, and specifically, forgiveness of this one person. This one person, my friend, is you.

We have piled so much onto our own shoulders. There are many things we intended to do that we didn't do, so many promises we made but didn't keep, and so many goals we set that we didn't achieve. Over time, they've piled up on us, and the weight can be crushing. You have to forgive yourself!

FROM THIS DAY FORWARD, MY HISTORY WILL
CEASE TO CONTROL MY DESTINY. I HAVE
FORGIVEN MYSELF. MY LIFE HAS JUST BEGUN.

I once broke my kneecap. It was the worst physical pain I had ever experienced . . . until I had an ear infection that landed me in the hospital. I wondered later why the ear was seemingly so much worse than the knee. The answer, of course, was that I could *mentally* amputate my knee. I was able to pull my mind away from the pain in my leg. But my ear? It was *in* my mind! I just couldn't get away from it.

The same is true of an unforgiving spirit. You cannot get away from it. It is impossible to fight an enemy that has a fort in your head. The only possible solution is to destroy the fort. Forgive yourself. Now.

FORGIVE YOURSELF

We tend to be our own worst critic, and judgment is a double-edged sword. In order to liberate yourself to begin to forgive others, you must first forgive yourself.

Using shorthand or personal "code words," list the things you need to forgive yourself for right now.

BEGINNING ANEW

We now have the opportunity to begin anew, to drop the heavy weight of guilt resting upon our shoulders. Month after month, year after year, we've added to the load, and it's about to crush us. All the things we said we were going to do but didn't, the promises we made and didn't keep, the things we shouldn't have done but did anyway have piled up, and it's just too much for one person to bear. The guilt has turned into resentment, the resentment has turned into anger, and the anger, in its various forms, is taking over our lives.

For many of us, our greatest enemies have been ourselves. Every mistake, every miscalculation, every stumble we make is replayed in our minds. Every broken promise, every day wasted, every goal not reached has energized the disgust we feel about our predicament. This dismay develops into a paralyzing grip. When we disappoint ourselves, it sets in motion a continual cycle of disappointment. It's true. It is impossible to fight an enemy living in our heads.

Forgive yourself. Begin anew. The simple act of forgiving yourself will change your life! You will be positioned to become the person you want to be when you finally ditch the weight of guilt and shame you've been piling on for years. Forgive yourself. Your family's not mad at you. Your friends aren't mad at you. I'm not mad at you. God's not mad at you. *You* don't need to be mad at you either. Let it go. Forgive yourself and begin again.

From this day forward, your history needs to stop controlling your destiny. Your life has just begun! Your forgiveness is valuable only when you give it away. By the simple act of forgiveness, you can release the demons of your past and create a new beginning for yourself.

Forgive the people who don't ask for it. Forgive yourself. From now on, your act of forgiveness will free you from unproductive thoughts. Your bitterness, resentment, and anger will be gone. It's time to begin again.

"I will greet each day with a forgiving spirit."

THE APPRECIATION LETTER

The purpose of this letter is to appreciate and free yourself from whatever you've been harboring against yourself. Commit to releasing something that you don't need to hold on to any longer. Example:

> Dear [your name],
>
> I've missed you. It has been too long since I've seen the fun, happy person I know you to be. So now I want to ask for your forgiveness about something. You will remember, it was five years ago . . . [describe the event]
>
> In closing, I want to acknowledge that you are one of the most special people in the world. These are the things that I appreciate about you . . . [list them]
>
> Thank you for magical moments that you create for so many. The ripples that you create by the way you live reach many more than you could ever know . . .
>
> > Love,
> > [your name]

Now it's your turn. Draft an appreciation-forgiveness letter to yourself.

REAL TRAVELER PROFILE:
NORMAN VINCENT PEALE

Dr. Norman Vincent Peale was a minister and an author of forty-six books, which have been translated into forty languages, including the perennial inspirational classic *The Power of Positive Thinking*. Along with his wife, Ruth Stafford Peale, he started a magazine called *Guideposts*, which is enjoyed by more than fifteen million monthly readers. More than thirty-one million copies of his inspirational booklets have been distributed over the years, and he maintained a full speaking schedule until his death in 1993. Peale received twenty-two honorary doctoral degrees and was one of the few private citizens in history to be honored in a White House ceremony when President Reagan presented him with the Presidential Medal of Freedom.

Norman Vincent Peale said, "When God wants to send you a gift, he wraps it up in a problem, and the bigger the gift that God sends you, the bigger the problem." It's easy to assume that the man who wrote *The Power of Positive Thinking* didn't have to worry about positive thinking. We figure that the author of a book that has sold thirty million copies to date must have had it easy, right?

Here, then, is the great letter I received from a man whose very life embodied the Compassionate Decision. It is a story that will surprise you—and one I am certain very few have heard.

Dear Andy:

I suffered rejection when I wrote a book called *The Power of Positive Thinking*. Actually, I wanted to call it The Power of Faith, but my publisher insistently demanded that I change the title to a phrase . . . [from] the book, "The power of positive thinking."

It soon, to my surprise, hit the bestseller lists; in fact, it was on the *New York Times* bestseller list for 186 weeks, which at that time was a record. This projected me into the most vehement criticism I ever received. I considered the book a vitally Christian book, but some ministers castigated me as an archconservative, a tool of capitalistic interests, who was turning Christianity into a way to get rich. One bishop, a scholarly and gifted man, usually dispassionate and objective, became quite intemperate in his attacks on the book and upon me personally. Many ministers even preached against some terrible thing labeled "Pealism." And one distinguished pulpiteer called my work a perversion of the Christian religion. This hue and cry became so violent that I actually wrote my resignation from the ministry, though my church stood by me valiantly. I took a train upcountry to see my aged father who perceived that something was bothering me. And he, even in that remote area, knew of the scathing attack upon me.

So my father, sitting in his rocking chair, said, "Norman, you have always been true and loyal to Jesus Christ. You believe in and preach Bible truths. You have always been in the mainstream of Christianity, never following any temporary faddism. You have united the pastoral office with the best in the scientific and healing arts. You have blazed new pathways of positive thinking to counter the old destructive negatives. You are my son, and your old father who has known good men and not so good men for eighty years and more, both in and out of church, says you are a good and loyal minister of Jesus Christ." He was silent and thoughtful for a long minute. "Besides, and remember this, the Peales never quit. It would break my heart if one of my sons was a quitter, afraid to stand up and face any situation."

My father was a gentle-spirited man, and in all my life I had never heard him use any expression that included a swear word. Imagine my shock when he said, "And Norman, there's just one thing more."

"What is it, Dad?" I asked.

"Tell 'em to go to hell," he declared, to my astonishment.

Stepping into another room, I tore up my resignation and threw it into the wastebasket. Needless to say, I came away fortified in spirit. The book has sold upwards of twenty million copies worldwide and has become, in book statisticians' opinions, one of the few books in American history that has sold the most. The title has become part of the language and culture in not only America but the world.

A lady who was at one time president of the National Council of Churches, Cynthia Weddell, meeting a friend of mine, said, "How's Norman?" And the friend replied, "He is fine." And added, "He has outlived his critics." "No," said Mrs. Weddell, "he has out-loved them."

In every rejection you learn something, and I learned that if you just go about your business and love people and not hate anyone, you ultimately gain a victory. Now it so happens that very few people criticize me, wherefrom I deduce that perhaps I am slipping.

Cordially yours,

Norman Vincent Peale

Norman Vincent Peale
NVP:SEL

THE PERSISTENT DECISION

I WILL PERSIST WITHOUT EXCEPTION.

Great leaders—great achievers—are rarely realistic by other people's standards. Somehow, these successful people, often considered strange, pick their way through life ignoring or not hearing negative expectations and emotions. Consequently, they accomplish one great thing after another, never having heard what cannot be done. That is precisely why one should never tell a young person that something cannot be done. God may have been waiting centuries for someone ignorant enough of the impossible to do that very thing!

Your success with the other six Decisions rests on your ability and willingness to embrace and master the Persistent Decision. To persist without exception means to ultimately ensure success in your endeavors.

I WILL PERSIST WITHOUT EXCEPTION.

Knowing that I have already made changes in my life that will last forever, today I insert the final piece of the puzzle. I possess the greatest power ever bestowed upon mankind, the power of choice. Today, I choose to persist without exception. No longer will I live in a dimension of distraction, my focus blown hither and yon like a leaf on a blustery day. I know the outcome I desire. I hold fast to my dreams. I stay the course. I do not quit.

I will persist without exception. I will continue despite exhaustion.

I acknowledge the fact that most people quit when exhaustion sets in. I am not "most people." I am stronger than most people. Average people accept exhaustion as a matter of course. I do not. Average people compare themselves with other people. That is why they are average. I compare myself to my potential. I am not average. I see exhaustion as a precursor to victory.

How long must a child try to walk before he actually does so? Do I not have more strength than a child? More understanding? More desire? How long must I work to succeed before I actually do so? A child would never ask the question, for the answer does not matter. By persisting without exception, my outcome—my success—is assured.

I will persist without exception. I focus on results.

To achieve the results I desire, it is not even necessary that I enjoy the process. It is only important that I *continue* the process with my eyes on the outcome. An athlete does not enjoy the pain of training; an athlete enjoys the results of having trained. A young falcon is pushed from the nest, afraid and tumbling from the cliff. The pain of learning to fly cannot be an enjoyable experience, but the anguish of learning to fly is quickly forgotten as the falcon soars to the heavens.

A sailor who fearfully watches stormy seas lash his vessel will always steer an unproductive course. But a wise and experienced captain keeps his eye firmly fixed upon the lighthouse. He knows that by guiding his ship directly to a specific point, the time spent in discomfort is lessened. And by keeping his eye on the light, there never exists one second of discouragement. My light, my harbor, my future is within sight!

I will persist without exception. I am a person of great faith.

In Jeremiah, my Creator declares, "For I know the plans I have for you . . . plans to prosper you and not to harm you, plans to give you hope and a future" (29:11 NIV). From this day forward, I will claim a faith in the certainty of my future. Too much of my life has been spent doubting my beliefs and believing my doubts. No more! I have faith in my future. I do not look left or right. I look forward. I can only persist.

For me, faith will always be a sounder guide than reason because reason can only go so far—faith has no limits. I will expect miracles in my life because faith produces them every day. I will believe in the future that I do not see. That is faith. And the reward of this faith is to see the future that I believed.

I will continue despite exhaustion. I focus on results.
I am a person of great faith.

I will persist without exception.

THE HABIT OF QUITTING

The Persistent Decision is the key to the other six: "I will persist without exception." Without this particular Decision, the other six are meaningless. When you make and own this decision, the other six Decisions are certain to work.

Committing to the Persistent Decision means you accept responsibility. You constantly seek wisdom. You never stop being a person of action. You have a decided heart, without exception. You choose to be happy every single day. You greet each day with a forgiving spirit. Every single one of the other six Decisions hinges on your acceptance of the seventh: "I will persist without exception." It's the one that brings them all together.

I *really* love to watch football. I don't even care who's playing— I just love football. It amazes me that I love watching football so much. Football is a true passion, and yet, in the sixth grade, I hated playing. I wanted to quit so bad that I gave myself headaches. I hated the practices, the coach, and staying late after school until dark. But my dad would not let me quit. I couldn't believe it. "You started it and you're gonna finish it," he said.

Even my mother got on his case: "You know he has headaches. This is not for him. He obviously wasn't built for this. He's a skinny kid, and look at those big kids out there."

My dad replied, "He doesn't have to play next year, but he will finish what he started this year." My dad took me aside. "Son, I want you to know that persistence is a habit. And so is quitting. One of the greatest favors I can do for you is to make sure you have the habit of persisting and never develop the habit of quitting."

I never did develop the habit of quitting. It was simply not accepted in my family. Once you started something, you finished it. If I signed up to sell seeds door-to-door, the other kids could turn their seeds back in, but I was selling every one of them. If I signed up to sell Christmas cards, every single card was going to be sold. "You may be selling them in May, Andy, but you will sell every one of these cards," my dad would tell me. He wanted me to understand that every significant thing I would accomplish in my life would be hard and would require persistence.

This was just something expected in my house, and I'm so grateful for it today. Every single day, I watch people cave on stuff that I know if they had just stuck to it, they would see great things. Persistence opens doors in life you've always dreamed about.

. . . WITHOUT EXCEPTION

It's easy to shrug off the Persistent Decision: "Well, duh! Who hasn't heard that before?" We've all heard we have to persist—we shouldn't give up. The unique twist is the last part: I will persist *without exception*. "Without exception" is what everyone tends to leave off.

When you persist without exception, miracles occur. You find a way where there is no way. Anytime you make a statement that you're going after something big—that you're going to do something unusual, something great—and the reward is also big, it's going to be hard. There is only a big reward for things that are tough to do. If it were easy, everyone would be doing it, and the reward would be small.

HOW LONG MUST A CHILD TRY TO WALK
BEFORE HE ACTUALLY DOES SO? . . . HOW
LONG MUST I WORK TO SUCCEED BEFORE I
ACTUALLY DO SO? A CHILD WOULD NEVER ASK
THE QUESTION, FOR THE ANSWER DOES NOT
MATTER. BY PERSISTING WITHOUT EXCEPTION,
MY OUTCOME—MY SUCCESS—IS ASSURED.

Anytime you go after something big, a time will come when it seems obvious to everybody that it's "over"—it can't be done. It may even seem obvious to you that it's over. If you get to that point and you have persisted, then others will tell you that it's okay to quit—because you've persisted. You hung in there, and you can quit with a clear conscience with encouragement from people around you because you gave it your best shot: "You tried. Lord knows you tried. We've watched you work. You're killing yourself! It's time to quit, honey. It's okay." People will encourage you to quit if you've persisted because society no longer holds a penalty for quitting . . . as long as you persist a little bit.

However, if you persist *without exception*, you will have to find a way where there is no way. And that is when miracles occur. Anytime you hit the wall, anytime you come to the end of the road, what you're lacking isn't money, mentorship, or time; you're lacking an idea. That's all—an idea.

I can't tell you how many times I've worked with people who have come to that point. They'll say, "It's just over. I know it. I understand *persist without exception*, but I think this might be the case where . . ."

I'll reply, "Well, what have you done? What have you tried?"

"We've tried everything. We've exhausted every possibility. There is nothing that could be done that we haven't tried. We just . . ."

"I know that there's nothing else you could possibly do. You don't know where else to turn." (This is a great little game you can play with yourself.)

> REASON CAN ONLY GO SO FAR—FAITH HAS NO
> LIMITS. I WILL EXPECT MIRACLES IN MY LIFE
> BECAUSE FAITH PRODUCES THEM EVERY DAY.

"That's right, that's right. We don't know where else to turn."

I'll reply, "I know you don't know, but if you *did* know the next move you would make, what would you do? If we were pretending, what would you say the next move might be?"

"Well, if I did know, I would probably do . . ."

And I'll say, "There you go. Do that!"

Remember . . . even when you are in the "deepest woods," you are only lacking an idea.

A COMMITMENT TO PERSISTENCE

I have a friend with whom I have lunch occasionally. He's a little older than I am, but he played football as a kid too. He was better than I was, and his dream was to play professional ball. He was a quarterback all the way through high school, and he even got a scholarship to play college ball.

But his dream of playing in the NFL, the National Football League, did not looking promising when he injured his back and didn't play in his senior year. By the last round of the NFL draft, the anxiety and disappointment were just crushing. Finally, the phone rang. One team had made him their choice in the final round . . . and at that time the NFL drafted *seventeen rounds*!

He was so happy; he would have signed for practically nothing. And, in fact, he did—$6,500. Of course, making the team was going to be the toughest challenge. He was competing against four other quarterbacks, but he wanted this more than anything in the world.

> LET ME TELL YOU THE SECRET THAT
> HAS LED TO MY GOAL. MY STRENGTH
> LIES SOLELY IN MY TENACITY.
>
> —LOUIS PASTEUR

He spent the weeks before his first training camp getting into shape and refining his passing skills. He threw thousands of balls through an old tire hung from an A-frame at his in-laws' house. And although his friends and family members were proud of him, they didn't really expect him to make the team.

In July, when he reported to camp, he was ready but scared to death. It was obvious the coaches didn't really expect him to make the team. When the jerseys were given out for the first photo session, they didn't even give him a quarterback's number. (In fact, if you get a rookie card of this guy, it shows him wearing number 42.)

Training camp was tough, and the competition was fierce, but his early preparation paid off. His confidence helped him perform well in scrimmages and preseason games until, with the final reduction of the squad, he was given a new jersey—number 15. He'd made the team!

Over the next three years, he sat on the bench and watched the team struggle through three of the most dismal years in the history of the franchise. They went through two coaching staffs; morale was horrible.

In his fourth year, in a bold move, the team hired a little-known assistant coach to be the head coach of the team. Nobody had ever heard of this guy. It turned out this new coach had traveled a similar path as my friend. He had come up through the ranks. He had never been a good player, but he loved the game so much he wanted to coach.

Some people thought this new leader was too volatile for the coaching profession. Many people said he couldn't relate to the players because he was wound too tight. He was given the opportunity to coach fairly late in his life, and then only because the team was so bad. My friend recalls, "If I thought it was tough to make the team, proving myself to this coach was even tougher."

My friend was a quiet guy, and the coach wasn't impressed with him. But he was impressed with his work habits, his stability, his confidence, and his ability to persist without exception. The coach saw a little of himself in my friend—not the greatest natural talent, but he had an innate inability to back down or quit.

In my friend's fourth year, the starting quarterback went down with an injury. My friend was ready. This was what he had worked so hard for! He went into the game and brought the team back from behind. After that game Bart Starr became the starting quarterback for the Green Bay Packers.

Vince Lombardi, that little-known coach, and Bart Starr led the Packers to one of the greatest all-time records in the history of the NFL. At one point they won five championships in seven years, including the first two Super Bowls, and Bart was named Most Valuable Player in each of those games. Bart was named the Player of the Decade in 1970, and has also been inducted, along with Vince Lombardi, into the Professional Football Hall of Fame.

YOU MUST KNOW IN THE GAME OF LIFE,
NOTHING IS LESS IMPORTANT THAN THE SCORE
AT HALFTIME. THE TRAGEDY OF LIFE IS NOT THAT
A MAN LOSES, BUT THAT HE ALMOST WINS.

Today Bart lives in Birmingham with his wife, Cherry, and his children and his children's children. He's been just as successful in business and in his personal life as he ever was on the football field. Bart will tell you that a large degree of his success has come from developing the habit of persistence without exception.

BECOMING A FORCE OF PERSISTENCE

You've done an excellent job so far defining what you want your life to be like and identifying the obstacles you had unknowingly allowed in your path. We all know how new obstacles and challenges tend to show up (even after we've clarified what we want). For this reason, we must arm ourselves with the tools and understanding to overcome obstacles so they don't become excuses for quitting.

Right now, define a powerful set of beliefs for yourself that you can call upon in your moments of need. Identify three core internal obstacles that often stand in your way. Perhaps you identify yourself as a procrastinator and you put off taking action. Or maybe you tend to let fear guide your actions and decisions. List three of these personal limiting obstacles.

Next, in the form of affirmations, write down the attributes you are committed to that are aligned with your persistent spirit. For example, next to the procrastination obstacle you may write, "I am committed to achieving my objectives" or "I will see this through. I am guided toward my vision." For the fear obstacle you can say, "I am bound by nothing. With persistence, I can achieve anything" or "With faith and courage, I persist until I succeed."

> Write them down in your journal and on a note card you can carry around with you. Remind yourself of your new affirmation every time you find your old obstacle presenting itself.

FAITH OR FEAR

So what is the difference in people? When faced with struggles, why is it that one person quits and another keeps going?

As Gabriel asks in *The Traveler's Gift*, "Does faith guide your everyday actions and emotions? Or does fear guide what you do?"

One or the other drives us, and both emotions are an expectation for an event that hasn't come to pass, or a belief in something that can't be seen or touched. To have faith is to believe in the hopeful potential of what one has not seen, and the reward of faith is to have the potential manifest. The emotional energy of faith is uplifting. Fear, in contrast, is also to believe in the dark potential of what one has not seen, and the only reward of fear . . . is more fear. The emotional energy of fear is life draining. Fear can be used as a catalyst for action, or by default, it imprisons a person in a life of mediocrity.

A man of faith reaps perpetual reward, and a man of fear lives on the edge of insanity. Fear is a vapor—a myth—and if you think that fear is some kind of warning from above to keep you out of trouble, you can forget that. There's no instance in the Bible that says fear is from God. Fear disrupts you and keeps you from your goals, dreams, and destiny. Fear and worry are interest paid in advance on something that may never come to pass.

Through the years, I've discovered that it's often the smartest people who are most susceptible to fear in the first place. I couldn't figure out why that is until I finally realized that fear is imagination run amok. What you fear doesn't even exist—it is the misuse of the creative imagination God has placed in you. And in the lives of these creative, intelligent people, somehow fear jumps into the mix and shuts down any possibility of moving toward their goals and dreams. It stops everything. The word *worry* is derived from an Anglo-Saxon term meaning "to strangle" or "to choke off." Worry and fear choke off any creative flow or intelligent movement that people might have otherwise had.

Ignore fear. Cast it out of your life. There is no reward for fear. The reward is in faith and in seeing what you have believed come to pass.

"I will persist without exception. I am a person of great faith."

THE DOORWAY BEYOND FEAR

Ralph Waldo Emerson said, "Always do what you're afraid to do."

What are the closed doors in your life? Many times, they stand as a limitation you've created in your mind. Your very limitations are segues to your dreams. If you will confront those limitations and deal with them rather than fear or avoid them, you will transcend them to experience unlimited possibilities for your life.

I have a friend named Erik Weihenmayer. Erik is one of the most amazing people I have ever known. He was born with a rare genetic disease, and by age thirteen, he was blind. At first he was aggravated, scared, and bitter. He could have decided the world was a terrible place to live and given up. He could have believed that God dealt him a horrible hand. Instead, Erik took his handicap and did what many said was impossible—he turned his blindness into a powerful tool that would allow him to live the life of his dreams.

ALL MEN ARE DRIVEN BY FAITH OR FEAR—
ONE OR THE OTHER—FOR BOTH ARE THE
SAME. FAITH OR FEAR IS THE EXPECTATION
OF AN EVENT THAT HASN'T COME TO PASS
OR THE BELIEF IN SOMETHING THAT CANNOT
BE SEEN OR TOUCHED. A MAN OF FEAR LIVES
ALWAYS ON THE EDGE OF INSANITY. A MAN
OF FAITH LIVES IN PERPETUAL REWARD.

Erik loved sports. But what sport can a blind guy play? He began with wrestling and became one of the high school team's star wrestlers. At sixteen, Erik discovered his passion for climbing. He was an active skier. He became a marathon runner, a skydiver, and a scuba diver. He loved adventure and chose to do the things that pushed him beyond what anybody else thought a blind man could do.

Early on, Erik decided he would use his handicap to live a life of growth, expansion, and risk. He chose to move beyond the retreat, fear, and limitations of his blindness. Instead, Erik challenged himself to grow enormously and to move beyond the black door of his handicap.

Was Erik always a world-class climber? Not at first. As a blind boy, he was angry. He fought the cane. He fought learning Braille. He fought anything that would label him. "I didn't want to be known as the blind kid," Erik recalls. "I wanted to be known for doing or being something cool."

For a while he floundered emotionally and academically; he flunked math his freshman year of high school because he had not learned Braille. But he bounced back.

Erik's passion for climbing was bigger than any disability or fear. Experiencing nature so tactilely, feeling the different textures of the rocks, sensing the wind blowing off the side of the mountain, listening to the sounds—for a blind person, it was sensory over-load, and Erik loved it! Fear was always there for Erik. It will be there for you, too, but Erik chose to use his fears constructively.

FEAR IS A POOR CHISEL WITH WHICH
TO CARVE OUT TOMORROW.

Erik was on the cover of *Time* magazine as the first blind person—and one of the few of any kind of person—to climb Mount Everest. When Erik went after Mount Everest, he knew that 90 percent of the climbers who attempted to reach the summit do not succeed, and many don't come back alive.

Did you know that more than 10 percent of the people who have attempted to climb Mount Everest have died? Would you get in a car if you knew you had a one in ten chance of dying? Yet, here was a blind man who climbed the highest peak in the world at twenty-nine thousand feet, with temperatures of up to thirty degrees below zero and winds exceeding one hundred miles per hour—not to mention the challenges of navigating an extremely rugged terrain that was always blowing, changing, falling, and shifting, with sharp ice, deep chasms, and dangerous crevices that must be traversed in order to reach the top. Literally, one false step could mean death!

What if you saw fear as a door that must be walked through—as Erik Weihenmayer does? He has climbed the highest peak on each of the seven continents. Erik acknowledges that sometimes he is scared and has to push through his paralyzing fear. "Rock climbing helps me to understand that a lot of life is just reaching out into the darkness," Erik muses. "It can be scary because you don't know what's there."

Erik believes that the hold he's reaching for is out there, even though he doesn't have a lot of time and will fall if he doesn't find it. His fingers will give out if he holds on too long, but he's hoping, praying, and believing that he's going to find what he's looking for. Erik understands that there are no guarantees, but he refuses to be paralyzed by fear.

"A summit isn't a place on a mountain," Erik reveals. "A summit is a symbol to remind us that, with the power of our minds, our bodies, and our souls, and with the power of these two small hands, we can transform our lives into something miraculous. When we join our hands with those around us, we can do more than transform our own lives. We can transform the very face of the earth."*

BREAKING THROUGH FEAR

What are some of the fears that keep you from achieving what you want, from participating in your passions? Write down the top three fears you have about life. These fears can affect your relationships, finances, career, or family. They can also affect your spiritual, emotional, and physical well-being.

Underneath each fear, write down two or three ways it manifests in the various areas of your life.

What would happen if you didn't act out these fears? What would you do instead? Write down one thing you would do to replace each fear with a different emotion the next time it showed up.

Are most of your fears real or imagined? The degree of risk and uncertainty you are able to handle in your life

---

* You can watch a fifteen-minute video conversation with Erik Weihenmayer on AndyAndrews.com.

will determine the level of fulfillment and reward you experience. Would anything be worthwhile if it wasn't tough, if it didn't carry risks, if it wasn't uncomfortable?

Reviewing each of your fears, what are two actions you can take in each area that would immediately diminish the fear holding you back? If Erik can scale Mount Everest, can't you work through some of your fears by taking focused, courageous, determined, deliberate actions?

What will it cost you if you don't take these actions? And when, specifically, will you take these actions within the next twenty-four hours?

TRUE RAINMAKERS

In Australia there is a story about a tribe of Aboriginal rainmakers. This particular tribe of rainmakers always made it rain. Now, Aboriginals are known for their rain dances, but some tribes were more successful than others, and word got around that this particular tribe was always able to make it rain. When the white communities were in trouble due to drought, they began to call this particular tribe to do their rain dance. On one such occasion, the leader of the white community went to the king of this renowned group and said, "Why is it that every single time you dance, it rains?"

The king replied, "It's very simple, actually. We dance till it rains."

Hanging in there, staying the course, and waiting for the success to happen is your best strategy! Do you know you cannot fail at whatever you've chosen to do? The only way you fail is if you quit. Failure and success are totally in your hands!

AN ATHLETE DOES NOT ENJOY THE PAIN
OF TRAINING; AN ATHLETE ENJOYS THE
RESULTS OF HAVING TRAINED.

Some people might say, "You'll never make it; it'll never happen. Why are you wasting your time?"

You've got to remember that one day, somebody's going to be wrong, and somebody's going to be right, and it's going to be really obvious to everybody who's who. Let those words wash over you. You're totally in charge. You have not failed until you quit. "I will persist without exception."

CREATING YOUR PRIVATE CHAMBER FOR RESULTS

To employ the Persistent Decision, it is helpful to find ways to move toward your goals more effectively. For example, you may have a specific project you're trying to plan, such as a long-overdue vacation for you and your spouse. Even though you often think about doing this, something always comes up: the phone rings, an e-mail dings, your cell phone vibrates, your child screams for help with math homework, dinner is ready, and then you are tired and need to sleep.

Life is demanding, and it's easy to get swept away in a never-ending sea of tasks and ongoing actions. Sometimes it's necessary to close your doors (temporarily), shut off your e-mail program, and turn off your cell phone so you can work on a goal that's important to you.

Select a goal you've identified in an earlier Decision

> exercise and schedule time to work on it. The time should be viewed as sacred and nonnegotiable—just like an important business meeting.

The Unlucky Traveler

Henry Wadsworth Longfellow said, "Perseverance is the great element of success. If you only knock long enough and loud enough at the gate, you are sure to wake up somebody."

Probably the best story I could tell you about perseverance in my own life has to do with that book that I've been referencing frequently, *The Traveler's Gift*. So many people assume because it was the *Good Morning America* Book Club selection and on the *New York Times* bestseller list, the book was a no-brainer for the publishing world and was accepted right away. That's not even close to the case!

When I completed the manuscript for *The Traveler's Gift*, I was convinced it was the best work I had ever done. I just couldn't convince anybody else. I couldn't get a publisher to publish this book. It took three years, three different literary agents, and fifty-one rejections from the biggest publishers in the world.

Now, that shook me a bit. People would be amazed to know how many times I've locked myself in my room and read my own manuscript. Because of the Persistent Decision—the seventh Decision—I knew I could not fail. I knew this book would be published if I just stayed the course.

Friends would read the manuscript and say, "This book changed my life," and then publishers would read the manuscript and say, "We don't get it. Pass."

Month after month, and what turned into year after year, I could not get this book published. Of course, something was happening in the background that I could not see. I knew there were reasons things happened as they did. I can see some of the reasons now. But at the time, it was frustrating!

I kept working and kept waiting, tempted by detours, but knowing I had to stay the course. Finally, a company that had already turned *The Traveler's Gift* down published it. Part of persistence is trusting you will find a way where there is no way!

How did I do it? I found someone more powerful than a publisher—the publisher's wife. We were at a dinner party one night, and I made sure we were seated across from the publisher and his wife. I knew at some point in the evening, someone would ask, "So what do you do?"

And someone did.

"Well, I'm working on a book," I replied, and I laid out the story.

"Wow, I'd love to read that sometime," the publisher's wife responded.

"I have a manuscript in the car," I said. "This is just for you, now. Don't let him read it," I added, pointing to her husband, the publisher.

We laughed, and that was the beginning of finally publishing the book. I found out later that she and her husband stayed up all night reading the manuscript. She stayed up all night reading, and he stayed up all night because as she read, she often elbowed him, saying, "Hey, listen to this part."

A week later we had a deal on the book. Persisting without exception. Amazingly, when you persist without exception, miracles happen!

In spite of all the publishers turning it down, we succeeded, and this publisher was the place it needed to be. The timing was right. When I saw Diane Sawyer stand up on national television—on *Good Morning America*—and hold up *The Traveler's Gift* and say, "This is a book that America needs at this time," it occurred to me that when I wrote the book, our country wasn't in the turbulent, uncertain aftermath of 9/11 and did not have the same needs. What I perceived as rejection or delays was really divine orchestration for the right time.

One day I was talking to a group of people after a speaking engagement. A lady approached and told me she had written a book that she was having a tough time getting published. In fact, after a year, more than twenty publishers and agents had turned her down. I said, "Well, let me ask you something: does knowing that *The Traveler's Gift* was turned down for three years with fifty-one rejections help you feel more encouraged?"

She said, "Actually, yes. No offense, but yes. It does make me feel better knowing you were turned down a lot more than I have been."

I replied, "Well, there you go. There's another reason for me to have persisted through my rejections—to be able to encourage you. I would never have chosen it, not in a million years, but I was allowed to go through this process, to prove my persistence, and to hang in there to tell you my story to encourage you."

PEOPLE OF PERSISTENCE

Thomas Jefferson said, "Never fear the want of business. A man who qualifies himself well for his calling never fails of employment."

So what is success for you? A new house? A child? A certain job? A raise? Certainly you and I both agree that success doesn't happen by accident. You must know what you want and what you're willing to give in order to get it. Two things will be required: first, a decision, and second, consistent action and follow-through until you succeed.

What does follow-through mean? It means continuous, tenacious action toward your goal—intended, planned, effective action. You won't get anywhere by waiting for God to give it to you. Remember: He feeds the birds but does not throw the food into their nests! Following through—intending success—means relentless commitment to achieving your outcomes through drastic action. Many people fall into the trap of deciding on a destination or goal without the commitment to follow through. One or two actions typically won't give you the success to which you're committed. Massive, consistent action is what's needed to get you there.

> CONSTANT DETOURS DO NOT BRING A MAN INTO
> THE PRESENCE OF GREATNESS. DETOURS DO
> NOT BUILD MUSCLE. DETOURS DO NOT PROVIDE
> LIFE'S LESSONS. BETWEEN YOU AND ANYTHING
> SIGNIFICANT WILL BE GIANTS IN YOUR PATH.

There are a million stories of success, and they generally involve persistence. Unsuccessful people bail or quit. Successful people persist without exception. When you hear stories of triumph, if you're like me, you put yourself in them and you think, *What would I do in that situation?* Sometimes the stories are so traumatic you think, *Boy, I hope I could hang in there!*

Imagine a pre-pizza-delivery world. What if your dream was to open a new kind of pizza place in town that featured a guaranteed delivery service within thirty minutes of every order?

Your pizza place, because it was so different, struggled at first. Just as you begin to build momentum, your pizza place burned to the ground. Would you start again and stick with the dream that you had, knowing that you were on the verge of success? People had yet to accept the idea of having food delivered to their homes, but you were sure they would. Would you persist without exception?

Tom Monaghan did. He rebuilt his pizza place and then built another, and another, until Domino's Pizzas were literally all over the world.

What if you were a quarterback in high school and everybody said you could not play that position because you were left-handed and your throws were hard to catch because the ball came off your hands in a reverse spiral, spinning the wrong way? Would you persist in your dreams of playing quarterback on your high school football team? And deal with the critics again when you were going into college? And again before the NFL draft? Would you hang in there to become the NFL's Most Valuable Player, as the Oakland Raiders' Super Bowl champion and four-time All-Pro Ken Stabler did?

What if you were a singer and you were told that your voice was nasally and not particularly pleasing, and you were turned down by every major record label in the world—twice? Would you go around the block a third time and knock on doors again with another song and a smile on your face, the way Randy Travis did?

What if you had an idea for a new version of popcorn people had been eating for years? Would you spend forty years crossbreeding three thousand hybrid varieties of corn to perfect the exact moisture content in each kernel—13.5 percent—so that every single kernel would pop? Orville Redenbacher did.

All these people wrote to me detailing the rejection they endured and the persistence that finally won the day. I have their letters along with several hundred more. A myriad of exceptional stories support persisting *without exception*, past the temptation to quit when circumstances aren't favorable or when the doubters' voices drown out your dreams.

STRATEGIC PLANNING: MOVING TOWARD YOUR GOALS

Building momentum toward your goals helps you more effectively live the Persistent Decision. A solid strategy for results-planning can expedite the realization of your goals:

1. What is a goal you really want to make happen? Choose something you have wanted for a while, though it has been out of reach. Really consider what you want and why you want it.
2. With your goal in mind, brainstorm ways to move toward it. Write down any actions—big or small—to help you achieve your goal.

Now take at least one action in the next twelve hours to bring you closer to living your dreams! Schedule time each day or each week to move closer to achieving your goals.

EMBRACING A WORLD OF CRISIS

We all enjoy hearing success stories, sweetened by the struggles people go through to achieve them. When it's your life, however, sometimes doubt creeps in and life seems harder than expected.

You might be going through the worst time in your life—or you may know someone who is. Remember, you're not alone. We all are either in a crisis, coming out of a crisis, or headed for a crisis. It is just part of being on this planet.

If you're still breathing, your purpose on earth has not yet been fulfilled. There is a reason you're still with us. There's more fun to have, more success to enjoy, more people to encourage, more children to teach, more laughter to share. Your work is not done! You're only at halftime. It's time to take a breath, get up, and get ready to go again.

Beware of the temptation to detour! Distractions are everywhere: movies and television, music, and another universe on the Internet. Detours don't build muscle; they don't provide life's lessons. Detours will only distract you from greatness, and greatness is your destination!

Nelson Mandela said he was just an ordinary man who became a leader because of extraordinary circumstances. He ran away from his guardian to avoid an arranged marriage as a teenager and joined a law firm in Johannesburg as an apprentice.

Years of daily exposure to the inhumanities of apartheid, where being black reduced one to the status of a nonperson, kindled in him a kind of absurd courage to change the world. Instead of settling into the easy rural life he'd been brought up in, or even modest success as an attorney, he determined that his only future certainties would be sacrifice and suffering—he chose this to change others and their lives.

In the revolution to transform a country of racial division and oppression into an open democracy, Mandela demonstrated that he wasn't afraid. His real qualities of forgiveness, patience, and persistence, however, revealed themselves after he was released from prison. He served a twenty-seven-year sentence for leading a nonviolent strike and for his involvement in the African National Congress's resistance against the ruling National Party's apartheid policy.

Times of calamity and distress have always produced the greatest people. The strongest steel is produced from the hottest fire.

Wherever you are in your life at the moment, you are only at halftime. Yes, they ran up the score on you in the first half. You made some mistakes, but you're about to run out on the field again with the lessons you learned; you will play a different game! Nothing is less important in life than the score at halftime. The tragedy would not be that you lost; the tragedy would be that you almost won and quit.

Think back to the people profiled throughout this book, like Buckminster Fuller, Bob Hope, George Washington, Joshua

Chamberlain, Joan of Arc, Norman Vincent Peale, Amy Grant, and General Norman Schwarzkopf. They all had problems, just as you do, just as you *will*. Problems are the "black door" to your opportunities.

TIMES OF CALAMITY AND DISTRESS HAVE
ALWAYS BEEN PRODUCERS OF THE GREATEST
MEN. THE HARDEST STEEL IS PRODUCED
FROM THE HOTTEST FIRE; THE BRIGHTEST
STAR SHREDS THE DARKEST NIGHT.

Our problems represent opportunities to enlarge our territory. In *The Prayer of Jabez*, Dr. Bruce Wilkinson reveals the power of a little prayer. He explains that we must ask and seek to have our personal territories enlarged and expanded. Will you allow your territory to be enlarged?

Persist without exception. From this day forward you will believe in the certainty of your future. Fear has no place in your life. It's time to have faith! Believe in the future, and watch your future manifest.

TRANSFORMING PROBLEMS INTO OPPORTUNITIES

Problems are part of life. What are your three biggest problems right now? List them in your journal. Then answer the following:

- What makes them so big? Or why do you believe they are big?
- What could be great about each of these problems? List five reasons each of these three

> problems could be great. If one of your biggest
> problems is massive credit card debt, this can
> be positioned as a great opportunity for you.
> You can create a clear and measurable goal of
> eradicating all your credit card debt.
>
> - List a few ideas for dealing with these problems
>   right now.
> - List three creative solutions to handling these
>   problems.
>
> Next, choose your biggest problem and the best solution
> you can implement immediately, and do it. Remember,
> during times of trouble, we're not lacking money, time, a
> mentor, or a leader. We're only lacking an idea.

AN IDEA BACKED BY CEASELESS PERSISTENCE

For my first book, *Storms of Perfection*, I came up with the idea to
compile stories from "overnight successes" recalling their worst
rejection in life. I asked, "What was the worst time or the worst rejection you experienced in your life before you became successful?"

I wanted the letters printed on their letterhead, in their own
words, with their signatures at the bottom. It was a great idea! I
just couldn't get anybody to do it. I had to get turned down by four
hundred people before I finally had the fifty-two letters I wanted
for the book. And that wasn't the difficult part.

I went to William Morris, the talent agency that was repre-
senting me at the time—one of the biggest agencies in the world,
with literary departments in London, Berlin, New York, and Los
Angeles—and presented them with my idea and the fifty-two

letters, and they turned it down—as did numerous other agents and publishers.

Many people around me thought it was over, but I had an idea: I would publish the book. I didn't have any money, so I mortgaged my condo to print the books.

CIRCUMSTANCES ARE RULERS OF THE WEAK,
BUT THEY ARE THE WEAPONS OF THE WISE.

I had 10,000 copies—weighing tons—delivered to my condo. In my comedy routine, I started talking about the worst time in my life. Perhaps if you were encouraged by another person's worst time, your "worst times" wouldn't seem so bad. People started buying the books at my shows. We ended up selling more than 100,000.

At that point I went back to the publishers and gave them the news, assuming they would now want to publish the book. I figured it would be a no-brainer. Instead they said, "Wow, obviously we were wrong. We certainly missed the boat on that. But you've sold all the books you're going to sell."

After I had sold 200,000 books on my own, I went back to all the publishers with the same offer. And they had the same response. "What are the odds on us being wrong twice?" they said. "Obviously, we missed the boat, but now it really *is* over."

I didn't even go back to the publishers at 300,000 or 400,000 or 500,000 copies sold. At 600,000 copies sold, my manager and I thought, *You know; maybe this is okay. It's unfortunate that we didn't have any help, but we did get to keep all the money.*

REAL TRAVELER PROFILE: JOAN RIVERS

Joan Rivers was one of the biggest headliners in Las Vegas. She toured the country, playing to sold-out theaters, and had a nationally syndicated television program, *The Joan Rivers Show.*

When people find out that I toured as Joan Rivers's opening act for two years during that time, they all ask the same question: "What is she *really* like?"

Joan Rivers is one of the nicest, most generous people with whom I have ever had the privilege of working. She never refused to sign an autograph, and even when she was in a hurry, she took time to really talk to the people who stopped her. And she always had time for me as well. She encouraged me, she bugged me to get married, and she was constantly watching out for my money. "Make a sandwich in my dressing room, Andy," she would say. "Did you see how much hamburgers were at the hotel? Ride in the limo with me. Don't you dare pay for a taxi!"

I'll always be grateful to Joan—she set a wonderful example of how to treat people. The following letter from her exemplifies the Persistent Decision.

Dear Andy,

You want an example of one rejection in my life? Only one rejection?!! I'd be lucky to keep this letter to one page! As far back as I can remember, I wanted a career in show business. And as far back as I can remember, people were telling me no. On December 7, 1958, I walked into The Showbar in Boston. I was to be paid $125 for the week, two shows a night. I had already checked into the hotel across the street. It was a dirty, horrible place, but I didn't care. This was my first job.

I had already been turned down by every agent in New York when I found Harry Brent. He was the man willing to work with me, mold my act, and ultimately book me into The Showbar as Pepper January . . . "Comedy with Spice!" Things were really looking up . . . or so I thought. After the first show, the manager called me over. "Hey, Pepper," he said, "you're fired."

I was devastated. *Fired!* Fired from my first job! I went back to my crummy hotel room and collapsed. I literally could not stop crying. I cried as I stood under the shower in that filthy tub, my feet protected with socks, the curtain open so that the killer from *Psycho* could not stab me! Standing in that dirt-blackened tub, I no longer knew whether the thing inside me struggling to get out was talent or only an obsession. But I didn't give in.

Soon I was booked and fired from my second job. Harry Brent also left me, taking the "Pepper January" name with him. "Women comics I can find," he explained, "but a name like this is hard to come by!"

Meanwhile, I was back to square one. Let me condense this letter, Andy, by telling you that I tried everything and called on everyone. Very little worked and everyone said no.

My own mother said, "You have no talent. You're throwing your life away."

One of the most powerful theatrical agents in the business told me, "You're too old. If you were going to make it, you would have made it by now." The talent coordinator for *The Tonight Show* said, "We just don't think you'd work on TV." The verdict certainly seemed to be in, but I just couldn't quit.

I had no money. My office was a phone booth in Grand Central Station. I lived out of one small suitcase and slept in my car while my father threatened to have me committed to Bellevue. All in all, not an easy time. It did, however, serve to shape the determination and an inner strength I have called on in my life many times since.

Even as I write this, it is far easier to recall my successes than the failures I've experienced. We all tend to forget the tough times. Children especially, I believe, sometimes see success as a "lucky lottery ticket" that one chances upon. And that is why I think it important to note that in my case, I was thirty-one years old. Thirty-one years of hearing no. Thirty-one long years before the acceptance began. Even in my darkest moments, I knew instinctively that my unyielding drive was my most valuable asset. Perseverance, my dear, will always be just as important as talent.

Never stop believing! Never give up! Never quit! Never.

Joan Rivers

FINAL THOUGHTS ON THE SEVEN DECISIONS

Although these are some final words and reinforcement of what we've learned together, they merely represent the beginning for you. Each day that you commit to mastering the Seven Decisions, a deeper meaning will be presented. Each day you choose to live each Decision, a new world of higher levels of love, happiness, wealth, and laughter awaits you.

DO YOU REALLY MATTER?

I was in a hotel room a couple of months ago ironing a shirt, somewhat listening to the television that was on at the other end of the room. I heard an anchor on one of the network news shows doing a "person of the week" feature. I heard him say, "And so the person of the week is Norman Borlaug."

I put the iron down and ran to the television. I couldn't believe it: Norman Borlaug! The reporter continued, "Norman Borlaug, our person of the week, is credited with saving the lives of over two billion people on our planet."

I was blown away. I didn't know the guy was still alive—ninety-one-year-old Norman Borlaug. I knew who he was. Borlaug had hybridized corn and wheat for arid climates. He won the Nobel Prize because he discovered how to grow a specific type of corn and wheat that saved the lives of people in Africa, Europe, Siberia, and Central and South America.

Borlaug was being credited with saving, literally, two billion people on our planet. The reporter was misinformed, however; I knew it wasn't Norman Borlaug who saved the two billion people. It was Henry Wallace.

Henry Wallace was the vice president of the United States during Franklin Roosevelt's first term. However, the former secretary of agriculture was replaced for Roosevelt's second term in favor of Truman. While Wallace was vice president of the United States, he used the power of that office to create a station in Mexico whose sole purpose was to hybridize corn and wheat for arid climates. He hired a young man named Norman Borlaug to run it. So Borlaug got the Nobel Prize and person of the week, but wasn't it really Wallace who saved the two billion people?

Or was it George Washington Carver? Before Carver ever made his amazing discoveries about peanuts and sweet potatoes, he was a student at Iowa State University. There, he had a dairy sciences professor who allowed his six-year-old son to go with Carver on botanical expeditions on Saturday and Sunday afternoons. Carver instilled in him a love for plants and a vision for what they could do for humanity. George Washington Carver pointed Henry Wallace's life in that direction long before that little boy ever became vice president of the United States.

So when you think about it, it is amazing how George Washington Carver "flapped his butterfly wings" with a six-year-old boy and just happened to save the lives of two billion people and counting. So perhaps Carver should be person of the week?

Or should it have been the farmer named Moses from Diamond, Missouri? Moses and his wife, Susan, lived in a slave state, but they didn't believe in slavery, which was a problem for a group of psychopaths called Quantrill's Raiders, who terrorized the area by destroying property, burning, and killing. One cold January night, Quantrill's Raiders rolled through Moses and Susan's farm, burned the barn, and shot and grabbed some people. One of these was a woman named Mary Washington, who refused to let go of her infant child, George. Mary Washington was Susan's best friend, and Susan was distraught. Quickly, Moses sent word out through neighbors and towns and managed to secure a meeting with Quantrill's Raiders a few days later.

Moses rode several hours north to a crossroads in Kansas to meet four of Quantrill's Raiders. They showed up on horseback, carrying torches, flour sacks tied over their heads, with holes cut out for their eyes. Moses traded the only horse he had left on his farm for what they threw him in a burlap bag.

As they thundered off on their horses, Moses knelt and pulled a little baby out of that bag, cold and almost dead. He put that child inside his coat next to his chest and walked him home through the freezing night. He talked to the child, promising him he would raise him as his own. He promised to educate him and honor his mother, whom Moses knew was already dead. And he told that baby that he would give him his name.

And that is how Moses and Susan Carver came to raise that little baby, George Washington Carver. So, when you think about it, it was really the farmer from Diamond, Missouri, who saved the two billion people—unless . . .

The point is that we could continue this journey back through to antiquity. Who really knows who saved those two billion people?

Who knows whose actions at a particular time were responsible for changing the entire course of the planet—two billion people and counting!

And who knows whose future will be changed by your actions today and tomorrow and the next day and the next.

There are generations yet unborn whose very lives depend upon the choices you make because everything you do matters—not just for you, not just for your family, not just for your hometown. Everything you do matters to all of us—forever.

PIONEERING YOUR OWN LIFE

By mastering the Seven Decisions, you are becoming a pioneer of new and unknown territories—both inwardly and in the world at large. A pioneer is somebody who goes into previously uncharted or unclaimed territory with the purpose of exploring it—and possibly colonizing, settling, or selling it. Pioneers take their destiny and the destiny of future generations into their own hands. This commitment opens the door to an exciting adventure with new allies, new treasures, and new discoveries to be made about humanity.

Will people follow you? What are you doing that is different from the throngs of humanity? What trails will you blaze for others to follow?

Pioneering leadership requires responsibility. In embracing the Seven Decisions, you become a leader and steward for others. As you lead others to success and a life of their dreams, the life you seek and deserve will be revealed to you.

How are you contributing to the lives of others? What will attract people to you? The first territory a pioneer must conquer is the internal terrain: *Who would I have to become for this to happen? Who do I want to come with me?*

BECOMING A PIONEER

To chart your goals and dreams, answer these questions in your journal:

- Where am I going?
- Who must I become in order for these things to happen?
- What must happen in order for me to get there?
- Who do I want to come with me?
- What are the potential obstacles I must deal with right now and along the way?

THE OBSTACLES ON YOUR PATH TO GREATNESS

Overcoming obstacles, setbacks, and pitfalls is a requirement for navigating your path to greatness. You must be aware of the potential challenges that lie ahead—otherwise, you'll be sabotaged and blindsided throughout your journey.

Your first obstacles are within: fear and doubt. The secondary obstacles are the ones outside of you: other people and their criticism, doubts, weird looks, and rolling eyes.

> AVERAGE PEOPLE COMPARE THEMSELVES WITH OTHER PEOPLE. THAT IS WHY THEY ARE AVERAGE. I COMPARE MYSELF TO MY POTENTIAL. I AM NOT AVERAGE. I SEE EXHAUSTION AS A PRECURSOR TO VICTORY.

What are some of the most oppressing questions that come to mind when you think about your goals? *What if I fail at this? What if people laugh at me? What if I don't have what it takes to succeed?*

We all have doubt or fear patterns that limit us in some way when confronting our dreams. Don't feel bad about having them. Be aware of them. Bring them to your conscious mind.

Wouldn't it be great if we could live our lives as if we'd already achieved everything we set out to do? Have you ever taped a football game? Maybe it was the biggest game of the year, and you were just dying to see this game. You were avoiding everyone because you didn't want to hear how it ended. Just as you were walking inside your house, your neighbor called out, "Hey, did you see how we won right at the last second? That was incredible!"

Man, how frustrating!

Because it was the biggest game of the year, you watched the entire thing anyway, but it wasn't the same. When your team fell behind in the first half, you didn't feel that sick feeling in your gut. As your team entered the third and fourth quarters, there was no reason to yell at the television screen, "A few more passes!" "Just hang on to the ball!" You weren't afraid because you knew you were going to win. You weren't sure how it was going to play out, but you *already knew* you were going to win.

Can you live your life as if you have already won? You know there will be pitfalls. You know there will be difficult times ahead, but you're not going to get scared or angry. Why? Because you are going to win!

SUCCESS THROUGH FAILURE

If success in any endeavor is to be accomplished, then failure must be embraced as well. As you have already seen, failure is a constant in the lives of successful people and, in fact, is often a precursor to their success. Anytime we view failure as the "final word," we rob ourselves of an incredible future that might have been ours.

When as an engineer for 3M Corporation, Spencer Silver set out to create hyperbonding glue, his reputation was at stake. He had been the lead researcher on many successful adhesives that 3M had branded and sold in the past. This time, however, the "king of stickiness," as his coworkers called him, produced an adhesive that was flabby, weak, and consistently dry. Despite the laughter of his colleagues, Spencer noticed two distinct qualities of this particular failure: the adhesive could be used again and again, and it left no residue *on any surface* as it was removed.

> FAILURE IS THE ONLY POSSIBILITY OF A
> LIFE THAT ACCEPTS THE STATUS QUO.
> WE MOVE FORWARD, OR WE DIE!

Perhaps because of these two qualities, Spencer patiently (and with good humor) endured the workplace jokes and determined that he would share his discovery with everyone in the office. One of his coworkers, a man named Arthur Fry, sang in his church choir and was often aggravated by losing his place in the hymnal. Having heard about Spencer's failure, Arthur Fry saw an immediate use for an adhesive that could be removed easily, didn't leave a residue, and could be used repeatedly. Post-it Notes became a huge success! But first . . . they were a failure.

Failure is often the pathway to something greater than expected. In fact, you can reliably depend upon failure as a pathway to new perspectives and new ideas. So put the "agony of defeat" in its proper place . . . a place of honor! After all, the "thrill of victory" is just one more reward for the person who rightly sees failure as a learning experience, a mill for ideas, and an opportunity to prove to ourselves, and others, that we are adaptable, imaginative, and strong.

The Realm of Endless Possibilities

If we're driven by fear and doubt, we can't enjoy winning the game. Instead of asking, *What if I fail?* turn that fear-based question on its head: *What if I succeed?*

Who might I reach? What if I loved myself in spite of someone else's judgments? What if this marriage did work? Who would I have to become, and what would I have to do?

Life's real rewards—love, happiness, and contentment—come through our internal growth. When you stretch yourself, you grow, and life's rewards are attained through this growth. A life of growth will bring you never-ending fulfillment, and mastering the Seven Decisions will help you have that life, paving the way to unlimited possibilities.

Through your efforts, you must prove you are worthy of obtaining the goal you set out to achieve. Ultimately, this journey is about uncovering the deeper level of greatness God has placed within you. Will it take effort? Sure! It'll take every last bit of effort and energy you have to realize your potential.

WHEN YOU STRETCH YOURSELF, YOU GROW,
AND LIFE'S REWARDS ARE ATTAINED THROUGH
THIS GROWTH. A LIFE OF GROWTH WILL
BRING YOU NEVER-ENDING FULFILLMENT,
AND MASTERING THE SEVEN DECISIONS
WILL HELP YOU HAVE THAT LIFE, PAVING
THE WAY TO UNLIMITED POSSIBILITIES.

Zechariah 13:9 says, "I will bring you through the fire and make you pure. Just as gold and silver are refined and purified by fire" (author's paraphrase). The golden parts of you already exist. You just need to uncover them by bravely walking through the black doors of fear in your life. Walking through your fears will help you find your freedom. You may *believe* this, but you won't *know* it until you face your fear and remove its roadblocks so you can realize your natural greatness.

It seems so scary and foreboding to walk through our fears because they contain so much "unknown." What if there was a reliable method for breaking through fear? Would you follow this method if you knew doing so would turn your dreams and visions into reality? Lock these words into your mind and heart: *Do what you are afraid of.*

If you're afraid of death, volunteer in a nursing home or an assisted-living center for several hours a week. If you're afraid of rejection, ask the most important person in your neighborhood to lunch. If you're afraid of public speaking, take a course in public speaking or go speak at your local Toastmasters Club. If you're afraid of failing, do exactly the thing you are afraid to fail at doing. Fail miserably and discover all the opportunities that failure offers.

What will happen when you do what you're afraid of? You may feel uncomfortable at first. You may feel insecure or uncertain or even worthless, but doing what you fear is like peeling an onion: it will reveal layers of unnecessary baggage that you're carrying around with you. And as each layer presents itself, you can peel it off, expose the illusion for what it is (not real), and cast it away. On the other side of this experiment is freedom from fear, and the realization of your dreams!

An Endless Web of Decisions

What are the hidden forces at work in our lives, and how can we trace them? What effect do our decisions have on the rest of the world?

In 1980, Tim Berners-Lee was doing a six-month stint as a

software engineer at Cern, a European laboratory for particle physics in Geneva. He was noodling around, trying to come up with a program for organizing his notes.

He had devised a piece of software that, as he put it, "could organize all the random associations one comes across in real life and that brains are supposed to be so good at remembering but sometimes aren't."

He called it Enquire, short for Enquire Within upon Everything, based on an encyclopedia from his childhood.

Building on ideas in software design at the time, Tim fashioned a kind of hypertext notebook where words in a document could be linked to other files on his computer, which he could index with a number. (Remember, there was no mouse to click back then.) When he punched that number, the software would automatically pull up its related document. It worked splendidly and confidently—and nobody else could use this software. It would work only on Tim's computer.

SOONER OR LATER, EVERY MAN OF CHARACTER
WILL HAVE THAT CHARACTER QUESTIONED.
EVERY MAN OF HONOR AND COURAGE WILL
BE FACED WITH UNJUST CRITICISM, BUT NEVER
FORGET THAT UNJUST CRITICISM HAS NO
EFFECT WHATSOEVER UPON THE TRUTH. AND
THE ONLY SURE WAY TO AVOID CRITICISM
IS TO DO NOTHING AND BE NOTHING.

Tim wondered, *What if I want to add stuff that's on someone else's computer?* After he obtained permission, he would have to do the dreary work of adding the new material to a central database. An even better solution, he thought, would be to allow others to open up his document on their computers and allow them to link their stuff to his. He could limit access to his colleagues at Cern, but why stop there? *Why don't we open it up to scientists everywhere?* In Tim's scheme, there would be no central manager. There would be no central database and absolutely no scaling problems. The thing could grow crazy like a jungle. It would be open-ended and infinite.

He later revealed, "One had to be able to jump from software documentation to a list of people, to a phone book, to an organizational chart, or whatever." He cobbled together a relatively easy-to-learn coding system he called Hyper Text Markup Language—HTML. Of course, HTML has come to be the language of the Web—it is how Web developers put up most web pages that include formatted text, links, and images.

He designed an addressing scheme that gave each document a unique location, a universal resource locator, or URL. He devised a set of rules that permitted these documents to be linked together on computers connected by phone lines. He called that set of rules Hyper Text Transfer Protocol—HTTP.

And at the end of the week, Tim cobbled together the World Wide Web's first browser, which allowed users anywhere to view his document on their computer screens.

In 1991, the World Wide Web debuted with a coding system that brought order and clarity to information organization. From that moment on the web and the Internet grew as one—often at exponential rates. Within five years the number of Internet users jumped from 600,000 to 40 million. At one point it was doubling every fifty-three days.

Tim Berners-Lee, trying to organize his notes, literally changed the way we live. Tim Berners-Lee works in a cubby at MIT now, but he has changed the world. He didn't cash in on his "invention" like a lot of people would have. He's content to labor quietly in the background, ensuring that all of us can continue well into the next century able to *enquire within upon everything.*

24 Hours and Counting . . .

What you do today matters for all of us. What you don't do matters equally. Remember that our mistakes are in the past. We must forgive ourselves and move on. We choose what we want our lives to be about. What do you choose?

To unleash the greatest creative faculties that God has planted within us, live each day as if you only have twenty-four hours left on this earth. How would you act? How would you look? How would you get out of bed tomorrow morning? How would you have dealt with that crazy person who cut you off in traffic? How would you address your five-year-old differently? What would you say to yourself before you went to sleep tonight? What would you say to your spouse before you went to sleep tonight, or your parents?

---

24 HOURS TO LIVE

With your eyes closed, take fifteen minutes and quietly allow yourself to mentally peruse all the ideas, thoughts, and energy that you've gleaned from this book and your journal. Let your mind open to the possibility of a bright future.

Ask yourself, *Who would I like to become, and what would I like to do with the next twenty-four hours of my life?* If twenty-four hours of your life is all you have left, what are you going do? Take ninety seconds and, in your journal, write down every single idea that comes to mind.

Next, pick out your top three ideas and rank them in order of importance. Alongside or beneath these top three ideas, write why each is so important to you.

Finally, write down what you will do right now to move toward accomplishing these three things within the next twenty-four hours. Use your imagination, and remember, you have twenty-four hours to live!

A DIFFERENT CHOICE

Your whole life is nothing more than a canvas of choices. What one choice could you make right now to change your life in a significant and lasting way?

Know this: You are different from everyone else. On planet Earth, there has never been anyone like you, and there never will be again. Your spirit, your thoughts and feelings, your ability to reason—all of these things exist collectively only in you. Your eyes are incomparable—they are windows to a soul that is also uniquely yours. A single strand of your hair contains DNA that can only be traced to you. Of the multitudes that have come before you and the multitudes that may follow, not one of them duplicates the formula by which you are made. You are different from everyone else! You are special! You are chosen. The qualities, many of them rare, that make you one of a kind are no accident.

Why have you been created different and unique from everyone else? You have been made different so that you might make a difference. In some way, you are changing the world! Every choice you make and action you take matters. Every choice you do not make, every action you do not take, matters just as much. Millions of lives are being altered, caught up in a chain of events initiated by you this very day. You choose what chain of events you will initiate, whether you realize it or not.

Understand that you have been given everything you need to

act, and the choice is yours alone: *Beginning this very moment, you will choose wisely!* Never feel inadequate again. Do not dwell in thoughts of insignificance or be content with wandering aimlessly. *You are powerful. You matter.* You have the choice, and you *are* the choice. *You have been chosen to make a difference.*

LIVING THE HERO'S ADVENTURE

As the hero of your own adventure, you now stand at a crossroads. The decisions you make from here on out will determine your destiny—so choose wisely. Just as hundreds of thousands of fellow Travelers have used the Seven Decisions to transform their lives, you have the power to do the same. Integrate these Seven Decisions into your way of being with the world, and the adventure will transform *your* life.

The Responsible Decision: The buck stops here.
The Guided Decision: I will seek wisdom.
The Active Decision: I am a person of action.
The Certain Decision: I have a decided heart.
The Joyful Decision: Today I will choose to be happy.
The Compassionate Decision: I will greet this day
    with a forgiving spirit.
The Persistent Decision: I will persist without
    exception.

With all that you've learned as you've read this book, what new shifts within yourself have you already begun to identify? What's changed? How are you different? How are you better prepared to play the hero's role and positively affect humanity? Write these distinctions in your journal.

A DESTINY WITH SUCCESS MEDITATION

The following is a reminder you can read aloud daily after you've completed all the exercises in this book. This meditation is designed to help reinforce everything you've learned. Read it aloud every morning upon arising and each night before retiring to bed for the next twenty-one days. Please feel free to edit or change the wording where applicable.

———————

I'm going to be the parent I've always wanted to be, the son or daughter I've always wanted to be, and I'll be the greatest friend in the world. I'll be a leader people look to in times of distress.

My destiny is assured. I have accepted responsibility for where I am, and I understand what I need to do to move forward in my life. *The buck stops with me.*

I'm on a constant search for wisdom, through my associations and the books I read. I understand that a year from now, through the people with whom I associate, the books I have read, and the choices I have made, I can actually be a different person. *I am moving into my destiny with a servant's spirit.*

I choose to act now. *I am a person of action.* I am seizing this moment.

I have a decided heart, and I will move; my destiny is assured!

And I will move toward that destiny with a smile on my face because *I choose to be happy.*

THERE IS A THIN THREAD THAT WEAVES
ONLY FROM YOU TO HUNDREDS OF
THOUSANDS OF LIVES. YOUR EXAMPLE, YOUR
ACTIONS, AND, YES, EVEN ONE DECISION
CAN LITERALLY CHANGE THE WORLD.

I have a light heart because *I've forgiven everyone who has offended me*. And most important, I've forgiven myself. Life has truly begun again because I understand the principles that will guide me through the second half.

The second half is where I win! The future begins right now. *I will persist without exception.*

BIBLIOGRAPHY

Chapter One
The Quotations Page website. Thomas Edison quote, retrieved January 3, 2007, from http://www.quotationspage.com/quotes/Thomas_A._Edison/.

Chapter Two
Buckminster Fuller Institute website: http://www.Bfi.org/.

Chapter Three
Chamberlain, Joshua Lawrence. *Bayonet Forward*. Gettysburg, PA: Stan Clark Military Books, 1994.
———. *Through Blood and Fire at Gettysburg*. Gettysburg, PA: Stan Clark Military Books, February 1994.
Desjardin, Thomas A. *Stand Firm Ye Boys*. Oxford University Press, 2001.
"Kentucky Boy Scout to Meet President After Heroic Act." *Bowling Green Daily News* (February 7, 2003), retrieved January 17, 2005, from http://bgdailynews.com.
Monticello, The Home of Thomas Jefferson website, retrieved December 14, 2004, from http://www.Monticello.org.
Mulick, S. "Heroic Boy Helps Stop Blaze." *News Tribune* (August 16, 2004), retrieved January 15, 2005, from http://www.thenewstribune.com.
Persico, Joseph E. *My Enemy, My Brother*. Cambridge, MA: Da Capo Press, 1996.

Pullen, John. *The Twentieth Maine*. Alexandria, VA: American Society for Training and Development, 1980.

Shaara, Michael. *Killer Angels*. New York: Ballantine Books, 1987.

Chapter Four

Barnum, P. T. *Life of P. T. Barnum*. Whitefish, MT: Kessinger, 2003.

The Literature Network website, "James—The Holy Bible—King James Version," http://www.online-literature.com/bible/James/.

Pagden, Anthony, trans. *Letters from Mexico*. New Haven, CT: Yale University Press, 2001.

Chapter Five

Charlie Plumb Motivational Speaker and Author website. "Captain J. Charles Plumb Book Excerpts," http://www.charlieplumb.com/book-insights .htm.

Chapter Six

Mason, John L. *An Enemy Called Average*. Colorado Springs: Cook Communication Ministries, 2003.

The Forgiveness Project website, retrieved February 21, 2005, from http:// www.TheForgivenessProject.com.

Chapter Seven

An interview with Erik Weihenmayer, Homiletics Online website, retrieved May 20, 2005, from http://www.homileticsonline.com.

Time magazine website. "The Time 100," retrieved February 3, 2005, from http://www.time.com/time/time100/leaders/profile/mandela.html.

Weihenmayer, Erik. *Touch the Top of the World*. Reissue ed. New York: Plume, 2002.

Conclusion

Andrews, Andy. *The Lost Choice*. Nashville: Thomas Nelson, 2004.

My Prime Time website. "Special Feature: Celebrate Failure," by Ashley Ball, retrieved January 21, 2005, from http://www.myprimetime.com/play /culture/content/postyourfailure/index.shtml.

"*Time* Magazine's 100 Most Important People of the Century," retrieved February 13, 2005, from http://www.time.com/time/time100/scientist /profile/bernerslee03.html.

ACKNOWLEDGMENTS

I am blessed to be surrounded by friends and family who have become a team of which I am thrilled to be a part. If I can ever be perceived as a person who makes good and informed choices, it is only because of my reliance on these people's wise counsel. Thank you all for your presence in my life.

To Polly, my wife and best friend. You are beautiful, smart, and witty . . . after twenty-five years it is still a great combination.

To Austin (14) and Adam (11), our boys. You bring me joy and perspective. I never knew I could love so much.

To Robert D. Smith, my personal manager and champion. After thirty-four years together, you still amaze me every day.

To Duane Ward and the whole incredible gang at Premiere Speaker's Bureau: you are not just partners—you are friends.

To Gail and Mike Hyatt, who gave life to my career as an author.

To Reneé Chavez, my editor, whose careful eye and quick mind made this a much better book.

To Matt Baugher, my publisher at W Publishing Group, and to Joel Miller, who first helped conceive of this product.

To Todd Rainsberger, who helped shape the thoughts that became the words that led to this book.

To Sandi Dorff, Paula Tebbe, and Tommie McGaster. Without the effort, prayer, and attention to detail of these three people, my own efforts would not come to nearly so much.

To Glen Seale and Ted Seale, for making my office a place in which I want to write.

To Katrina and Jerry Anderson, Vickie and Brian Bakken, Sunny Brownlee, Foncie and Joe Bullard, Gloria and Bill Gaither, Michelle and Brian Gibbons, Gloria and Martin Gonzalez, Lynn and Mike Jakubik, Liz and Bob McEwen, Edna McLoyd, Mary and Jim Pace, Glenda and Kevin Perkins, Brenda and Todd Rainsberger, Kathy and Dick Rollins, Jean and Sandy Stimpson, Maryann and Jerry Tyler, Mary Ann and Dave Winck, and Kathy and Mike Wooley. Your influence in my life is undeniable, and your example is very much appreciated.

To Scott Jeffrey, the Bear Bryant of "life coaches," who took the words from my speeches and helped form them into a coherent narrative. His superior skill at bridging the contextual gaps, polishing, and refining were indispensable, and, Scott, you are "inexpendable" (don't edit me!). (ScottJeffrey.com)

ABOUT THE AUTHOR

Hailed by a *New York Times* reporter as "someone who has quietly become one of the most influential people in America," Andy Andrews is a best-selling novelist, speaker, and consultant for the world's largest corporations and organizations. He has spoken at the request of four different United States presidents and recently addressed members of Congress and their spouses. Zig Ziglar said, "Andy Andrews is the best speaker I have ever seen."

Andy is the author of the *New York Times* bestsellers *The Traveler's Gift, The Noticer,* and *How Do You Kill 11 Million People?* He lives in Orange Beach, Alabama, with his wife, Polly, and their two sons.

JOIN ANDY'S VIP E-MAIL LIST FOR FREE ACCESS TO:

- *Exclusive Online Resources*

- *Weekly Blog and Podcast Content from Andy*

- *Special Promotions*

- *and More*

Go to AndyAndrews.com to join for free!

To book Andy for corporate events,

go to the website or call

(800) 726-ANDY (2639)

The
NOTICER

*Sometimes, all a person needs
is a little perspective.*

The
NOTICER
RETURNS

*Sometimes you find perspective,
and sometimes perspective finds you*